LEONARD SWEET

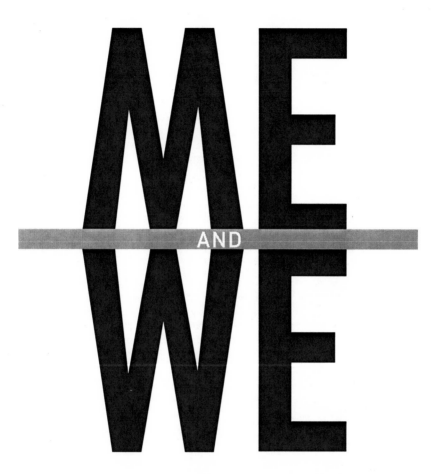

ME
AND
WE

GOD'S NEW SOCIAL GOSPEL

Abingdon Press
Nashville

ME AND WE:
GOD'S NEW SOCIAL GOSPEL

Copyright © 2014 by Abingdon Press

All rights reserved.

This book is printed on acid-free paper.

Library of Congress Cataloging-in-Publication Data has been requested.

ISBN 978-1-4267-5776-1

All scripture quotations unless noted otherwise are from the Common English Bible. Copyright ©2011 by the Common English Bible. All rights reserved. Used by permission. www.Common EnglishBible.com.

Scripture quotations marked (NRSV) are taken from the New Revised Standard Version of the Bible, copyright 1989, Division of Christian Education of the National Council of the Churches of Christ in the United States of America. Used by permission. All rights reserved.

Scripture quotations marked "NKJV™" are taken from the New King James Version®. Copyright © 1982 by Thomas Nelson, Inc. Used by permission. All rights reserved.

Scripture quotations marked (KJV) are taken from The Authorized (King James) Version. Rights in the Authorized Version in the United Kingdom are vested in the Crown. Reproduced by permission of the Crown's patentee, Cambridge University Press.

Scripture quotations marked (NIV) are taken from the Holy Bible, New International Version®, NIV®. Copyright © 1973, 1978, 1984, 2011 by Biblica, Inc.™ Used by permission of Zondervan. All rights reserved worldwide. www.zondervan.com. The "NIV" and "New International Version" are trademarks registered in the United States Patent and Trademark Office by Biblica, Inc.™

Scripture quotations marked (*"The Message"*) are taken from *THE MESSAGE*. Copyright © by Eugene H. Peterson 1993, 1994, 1995, 1996, 2000, 2001, 2002. Used by permission of NavPress Publishing Group.

Scripture quotations marked (AMP) are taken from the Amplified® Bible, Copyright © 1954, 1958, 1962, 1964, 1965, 1987 by The Lockman Foundation. Used by permission. (www.Lockman.org)

Scripture quotations marked (CEV) are from the Contemporary English Version Copyright © 1991, 1992, 1995 by American Bible Society, Used by Permission.

Scripture quotations marked (MNT) are from James Moffatt, The Holy Bible Containing the Old and New Testaments, A New Translation (Chicago: University of Chicago Press, 1922).

Scripture quotations marked (GNT) are from the Good News Translation in Today's English Version-Second Edition © 1992 by American Bible Society. Used by Permission.

Scripture quotations marked (NASB) are taken from the New American Standard Bible®, Copyright © 1960, 1962, 1963, 1968, 1971, 1972, 1973, 1975, 1977, 1995 by The Lockman Foundation. Used by permission. (www.Lockman.org)

Scripture quotations marked (AT) are the author's own translation/paraphrase.

14 15 16 17 18 19 20 21 22 23—10 9 8 7 6 5 4 3 2 1

MANUFACTURED IN THE UNITED STATES OF AMERICA

To Chuck Conniry
whose Micah 6:8 life inspires and illumines my life

"As for **me** *and my house,* **we** *will serve the Lord."*

—Joshua 24:15

Contents

Contents

Acknowledgments

All writers have an abiding theme, or obsession. As Phillip Larkin famously said, "Deprivation is for me what daffodils were to Wordsworth," although one wonders what Larkin was ever deprived of. This book reveals the abiding theme of my life: identity, as expressed in Jesus's haunting words to his disciples, "What do you more than others?"

Those closest to me have been drawn into my obsession—Thane, Soren, Egil, Elizabeth—and I am grateful to them for their good-spirited encouragement and forbearance of my daily dullness while writing this book. They were deprived of many more interesting "table talks" as I obsessed over these issues and tried to obtain their perspectives. My writing partner and editor Lori Wagner shepherded this book through its various stages, and I'm grateful to have someone with a poet's delight in language to whom I can entrust my thoughts. Betty O'Brien labored over portions of this manuscript, finding references when I couldn't and generally saving me from many instances of a surface clarity that tempts readers to skate over difficulties that only crack open later. During the final stages of this book, Betty's husband of forty-eight years and my friend Rev. Elmer J. O'Brien made his transition to our eternal home. Not a day goes by that I don't thank God for every remembrance of this librarian, author, bibliophile, minister, mentor, and friend.

In the course of writing *Me and We,* I came to a conclusion. Economics is not a science or an art. It is another word for politics. And the solution to our problems is not found in politics, the struggle of "means" over "ends." Our problems can't be wished away, whisked away, whisky'd away, or whistled away. Only washed away.

There are few people with whom I enjoy sharing such thoughts and debating with more than Chuck Conniry, vice president/dean of George Fox

Acknowledgments

Evangelical Seminary at George Fox University. Chuck thinks and feels, not just sees, in color. And for coloring my life with the vividness of Jesus, I dedicate this book to you, friend.

Leonard Sweet
Orcas Island, Washington State
August 2014 (in the midst of the one-and-only Sweet Family Reunion)

Introduction

House and Garden

We discover who we are in service to one another, not the self.

—Bono

For humans to be human, the chief developmental task of life is to find an identity. Fundamentally, that means a coming to terms with two simple words: *Me* and *We*. But simple isn't so simple. It is the thesis of this book that no one can be a Me without a We, that Me needs We to be, that a true Me/We must reside and rest in God's "House and Garden," that a Me/We gospel is for the world, and that a "we first" world requires a "me last" imagination.

In a way, the book that follows is summarized in parable form in "The Ship That Found Herself" by English poet, novelist, and children's writer Rudyard Kipling. This short story tells of a newly launched vessel setting out on her maiden voyage. Her timbers creak and groan against each other. She buffets her way through stormy seas. Gradually her component parts take more kindly to each other. Instead of being so many bits of steel and wood, she is a live and buoyant being. The spirit of the ship is born, and what was once born of matter now sails the open seas with a soul.

Four short quotes tell the whole story:

"For a ship [the skipper says] . . . is in no sense a rigid body closed at both ends. She's a highly complex structure o' various an' conflictin' strains, wi' tissues that must give an' tak' accordin' to her personal modulus of elasteec-ity. . . . Our little *Dimbula* has to be sweetened yet, and nothin' but a gale will do it."[1]

1

"You see," [the Steam] went on, quite gravely, "a rivet, and especially a rivet in your position, is really the one indispensable part of the ship." The Steam did not say that he had whispered the very same thing to every single piece of iron aboard. There is no sense in telling too much.[2]

"We have made a most amazing discovery," said the stringers, one after another. "A discovery that entirely changes the situation. We have found, for the first time in the history of ship-building, that the inward pull of the deck-beams and the outward thrust of the frames locks us, as it were, more closely in our places, and enables us to endure a strain which is entirely without parallel in the records of marine architecture."[3]

When a ship finds herself all the talking of the separate pieces ceases and melts into one voice, which is the soul of the ship.[4]

In this short book, we will look at the identity formation of Me and We in light of three of the world's greatest failings, each one of which goes directly to the genesis of the human problem: individualism, racism, and consumerism.

The world was created to be in relationship. Nothing exists by itself. This is why dividing society's problems into issues and agendas and "isms" only makes the problems worse. Individualism, racism, and consumerism are only a few issues that reflect our prevailing addiction to divide and fill. But they are not simple, solitary issues. They are interwoven into a complex fabric of other ills that infect society due to our fallen dreams and drives.

To talk about one or the other in this book is not to separate them out and magnify them but to see them as one of many symptoms of a sick body that is disconnected from God in ways that have caused bodily harm. To treat an illness organically, one must address problems of the whole organism— body, mind, and spirit—which is precisely what the first social gospel movement failed to do, and why we are calling this a "new" social gospel.

How and Where the Old Social Gospel Failed

The social gospel is known as a turn-of-the-twentieth-century movement that sought to bring about the kingdom of God on earth by constructing Christian social institutions and systemically transforming social structures.

- To a church that was operating on the principle "change hearts, change world," the social gospel countered "change world, change hearts."

- To a church that magnified the unspeakable joys of heaven and muted the unbearable horrors of earth, the social gospel reversed the volume.

- To a church that resembled two shipwrecked people at one end of a lifeboat, doing nothing but watching those at the other end bailing furiously to keep the boat afloat, one saying to the other, "Thank God that hole isn't in our end of the boat!"—the social gospel countered, "We sink or swim together."

- To a church that fixated on the Me, the social gospel focused on the We—sort of.

And this "sort of" is the reason for this book.

The social gospel came and went. The movement's demise has been the subject of vast speculation and scrutiny, but it can be seen perhaps best this way: social gospelers tried to save an ailing turtle by switching out its shell, one embossed with the name of "Christianity."

Institutionalizing Is Not Incarnating

You thought I was going to say Jesus, didn't you? But the first social gospel movement was more about institutionalizing social Christianity than about incarnating a Jesus faith. Its naive view of sin and optimistic outlook on the betterment of human nature failed to look up close and see that evil is real and personal. Evil is not just impersonal systemic forces but hurting people hurting people.

I have dispositional optimism but experiential pessimism about the human condition. We humans seem to be capable of great kindness, so long as it does not cost us anything. The human condition is this: we are wanting to get much; we are willing to give little. There is an ineradicable, irreducible component of evil in the human heart that makes the finest and the worst tendencies coexist in every human being. The Final Solution is the center showcase in human sin and the history of atrocity, but it is only one chapter in a very long book. Even Christians at times can give evil a bad name.

When the story of religion in America for the past twenty-five years is written, there is one word that will jump out. It's a word that trips off the lips of those on both ends of the theological spectrum. That word is *justice*, which usually comes attached to this word: *social.*[5]

3

In many ways, the social justice movement is the contemporary equivalent of the social gospel movement, except this time it finds its most eloquent advocates on the evangelical side of the religious divide. It's as if evangelicals showed up a hundred years late to the social gospel party, and they are making many of the same mistakes that the first social gospelers made.

The opening line from an invitation to attend a conference with a long justice wish list read as follows: "'Social Justice' isn't the latest fad for the church, it IS the very calling of the body of Christ and the core message of the life of Jesus."[6] Right after receiving this invitation, as if to underline the linchpin status of social justice as the "core message" of Jesus and the extent of its reach, I sat in an Anglican pew on a summer Sunday in Cambridge, England, and listened as the preacher launched into a tirade of the pieties of justice, one of which was that Jesus as "God's Son" was better heard as Jesus, "God's Justice," or "God's justice entering this world." The more I heard this respected preacher, the more I thought of one of those DEA dogs trained to sniff out dangerous substances. The dogs are totally indifferent to anything else—beef, bones, rawhide—other than the smell of drugs. What this preacher was trained to sniff out of the Bible was justice. There was nothing else—no love, no faith, no mercy, no humor, no hope—only strategies for justice in a world teeming with injustices.

The term *social justice* was first coined by the Jesuit Luigi Taparelli (1793–1862) in the 1840s, but it has only been in the last thirty years that the phrase has become a sacred mantra and verbal tic. The perceived need for justice arises out of the sense that the world is not as it should and could be, and for that reason Aristotle made justice the most perfect virtue because it orients human actions toward others. Christian social justice is based on the belief that Jesus came to bring highest heaven to the lowliest places and lowest people on earth, and that God adjusted the scales of justice so that the meek and merciful inherited the earth. Jesus didn't spend his time talking about "God is like this," but "the kingdom of God is like this."

The problem with justice is that no one knows what justice is. Everyone knows what injustice is, but no philosopher in history has been able to satisfactorily define justice.[7] Even injustice is not easy to define, and most often subject to Justice Potter Stewart's "you know it when you see it" pornography test. One of the better definitions of justice may be this: Justice is what emerges in the struggle against injustice. Amartya Sen's *The Idea of Justice* (2009) argues that justice is not a philosophical category or principle (*niti*) at all but a practice (*nyaya*). Justice is a practical matter of dealing with injustice. Justice is asking "what is best to do in the here and now, given what can be done."[8]

In other words, we are back to Micah 6:8 where we are to love mercy and do justice, all the while walking humbly with our God. When you advocate for the "kingdom of justice" as the framing story of scripture rather than Jesus's life, death, and resurrection as the framing story, what you end up with is everything "social" and nothing "gospel." In the scriptures, the kingdom is never something you build or create. The kingdom is something you receive and enter, because Jesus *is* the kingdom.[9] Origen (ca. 185–254) called Jesus "the kingdom in person, auto-basileia."[10]

DNA contains all of the instructions for the perpetuation and reproduction of an organism: Jesus is the DNA of the church. Not justice. Jesus. Any attempt to see Jesus's understanding of the kingdom of God as a political movement or an apocalyptic regime or a social justice program—anything other than the revelation of God with a divine personality at its heart—is to put ideology in the place of faith, abstraction in the place of concretion, and a prosecutorial accusative punishment story in the place of a salvation and mercy story. When Jesus judges injustice, and exercises justice, he doesn't take blood, he spills his own blood. He identifies himself with the whole We—both the oppressed and the unjust oppressors. The church exists to grow communities of holiness, not justice. When the church starts to sound more like a hanging judge than an umpire and judge-and-juries everything it comes across, it is time to reboot.

Divine power has its chief manifestation in divine mercy.

—Thomas Aquinas, *Summa Theologica*

The rallying cry of "We want justice!" creates some pause for anyone who has ever read the history of Western civilization. Or the history of the church. Or who has ever visited the Guantanamo Bay (Cuba) detention center, whose entrance sign reads simply "Camp Justice." Humans are never more "the killing machine" than in the name of justice, in the pursuit of progress, or out of the passion of religious zeal for justice and God's kingdom. Machiavelli wrote *The Prince* to refute Cicero's claim that honesty is always the best policy. Does the Bible say lying is always wrong? Machiavelli claimed to be a Christian, and frequently referred to God and to heaven, especially in his correspondence. But for Machiavelli, religion was a set of ethical principles, self-imposed moral obligations, especially principles revolving around issues of justice.

If you want to see unthinkable, unspeakable evil, look in the face of communism and fascism,[11] which are different but were alike in viewing mass killing as a legitimate instrument of social justice and progressive engineering. Both constellations funneled religious myths, especially millenarian ones, in a modern, secular form.[12] We even have philosophers of killing who see it as a positive good for parents to kill infants suffering from Down syndrome or other inconvenient ("unjust") maladies, so that they can be "replaced" with better, more "just" human specimens.[13]

The church itself has a sordid history of embracing political movements based on their sweet talk about social justice. The most theologically complete social gospeler, Walter Rauschenbusch, went gaga over the Russian Revolution. He called it God's gift to the world as the best emerging model of peace and justice. What enabled the Nazis to co-opt the Lutheran Church and replace the cross with a swastika? Its professions of "justice for Germany" and "positive Christianity." One of Hitler's favorite sign-offs was "By fending off the Jew, I struggle for the work of the Lord."

The world is not the ground of our hope; it is the subject of our love and the object of our mission. Our hope is built on nothing less than Jesus and his promises. That is why we can protest the world as it is and press on for the world as it should be. Jesus challenged the assumption that "when things change, the world will get better." Rather, for Jesus it was "When I change, things will get better." He called on Zacchaeus, the crooked tax collector, not to reform the tax code of Rome but to come to himself and follow him. He called on the Samaritan women, not to reform the relationships between Jews and Samaritans but to come to herself and follow him.

Mercy without justice degenerates into dependency and entitlement. . . . Justice without mercy is cold and impersonal, more about rights than relationship.

—Robert D. Lupton, *Toxic Charity*

The Apostle Paul said that there are three things on which our whole world depends: faith, hope, and love. But the greatest of these is love.[14] The heart of God is not anger or judgment or punishment but steadfast love, "the love that moves the sun and stars" (in the closing lines of Dante's *The Divine Comedy*). Yet another witness, Saint Isaak of Syria: "Among all His actions there is none that is not entirely a matter of mercy, love, and compassion; this constitutes the beginning and end of all His dealings with us."[15] Mercy is not a weak virtue. Mercy was not a Greek virtue, and it is a challenge to find it even mentioned in ancient literature. Yet we are blessed in having a "merciful and faithful high priest."[16] A miracle is a reversal of the laws of nature and human nature. In other words, a miracle is a manifestation of God's mercy, not God's justice.

When Nelson Mandela emerged from prison after twenty-seven years, he did not seek "justice." Mandela sought "truth and reconciliation." Do we really want a messiah known for his "quality of mercy" or "quality of justice"— we who are morally complicit with every breath we take? Every choice we make is compromised: If you hear someone drowning ten feet away and you do nothing, are you culpable? Fifty feet? Five hundred feet? Five thousand feet? Five thousand miles, as seen on the nightly news? Justice is getting what you deserve. Mercy is *not* getting what you deserve. Grace is getting what you don't deserve. In the words of Dorothy L. Sayers, "When we demand justice, it is always justice on our behalf against other people. Nobody, I imagine, would ever ask for justice to be done *upon* him for everything he ever did wrong. We do not want justice—we want revenge; and that is why, when justice is done upon us, we cry out that God is vindictive."[17] As one of those to whom "much is given," which means "much will be required,"[18] I shall need one day to plead the mercy of the court.

It is reigning social justice orthodoxy that the deeper we go into politics, and the more we get involved in political action, the deeper our discipleship. The truth is that it is easier to live out one's faith in Las Vegas than in Washington, DC. There is no more challenging arena for a "lived faith" than in the political sphere. The gospel's call of discipleship is more radical than political action. Politics is not the communal actualization of grace but the human organization of power and cunning. We don't serve the cause of justice when we become politicians. By pointing people to the power of God, the claims of the gospel, we trust that the "lifting up of Christ" will open up spaces and release energies for change to take place, some of which will take political form in a variety of stripes and strikes. The end of political action is not bringing the kingdom closer but losses and crosses. Politics does not lead to success but to the cross, the ultimate protest against the status quo, the ultimate manifesto of what should be. That's where true politics ends up: at the cross.

System Sin at the Expense of Individual Sin

The first social gospel trained the church in systems thinking. To be sure, we cannot focus on individual sin at the expense of structural evil. But if you could fix all the systems of the world, you would still have to deal with the human heart. If we somehow could get rid of all the crimes against humanity, humanity would still commit crimes. This is what is behind the "cause fatigue" starting to plague young Christian activists, already world-weary from its insoluble problems.[19] What is wrong with humanity cannot be fixed simply by what is right with humanity.

Our humanity is contingent on the humanity of our brothers and sisters. . . . We rise above the animal together, or not at all.

—Chinua Achebe's credo

The human propensity for evil is not something patched on but woven into the very fabric of what it means to be human. Walter Benjamin said that every record of civilization is also a record of barbarism. "I've seen the meanness of humans till I don't know why God ain't put out the sun and gone away" says a character in Cormac McCarthy's *Outer Dark*.[20] A century earlier, Mark Twain defined *human* as "a creature made at the end of the week's work when God was tired." The emotional ecology of human life is so full of evil emotions and toxic thoughts that Fyodor Dostoyevsky, who came to despise religion but love Christ, could confess: "The more I love humanity in general, the less I love man in particular."[21] That's why Jesus came to humanize the soul, not to divinize it.

What Is Wrong Cannot Be Made Right by Human Goodness

This is the real Achilles heel of the first social gospel. Who were the greatest optimists about human nature in the nineteenth century? Karl Marx, who was convinced that a brave new world was coming; transcendentalists like Ralph Waldo Emerson and Henry David Thoreau; and social gospelers like Henry

George, Washington Gladden, Jane Addams, Josiah Strong, Shailer Mathews, W. D. P. Bliss, George D. Herron, Charles M. Sheldon, and most notably Walter Rauschenbusch, who collectively launched the progressive impulse in American culture long before there was a Progressive party. Blaming sin on society and downplaying individual responsibility, these social gospelers believed that once you improved material conditions, the spiritual conditions would improve perforce. In the words of historian and scientist Robert Fogel, who won the Nobel Prize for economics in 1993, "The Social Gospelers' effort to reform human nature, to crush evil, and to create God's kingdom on earth through income redistribution [and other structural initiatives] has failed."[22] Reinhold Niebuhr, who critiqued social gospel theology on its anemic approach to sin and antiseptic approach to grace, called "ironic evil" the tendency of our virtues to become our vices, our strengths to become our weaknesses, our wisdom to become our folly.[23] It is not insignificant that the social gospel movement ushered in the bloodiest and most brutal century in human history.

People are not categorically good or evil, with good coming from the good and evil from the evil. Good can come from evil, and evil from good. No one is wholly good or wholly evil. Goodness, wherever it comes from, glorifies God. The critics of Christianity are right by saying things like, "The increase of Christ's glory in the world has been accompanied by lies, opportunism, injustices, religious divisions and hatreds, torture and murder." But amid the horrors and errors, there are splendors. God's mission in the world is ongoing, and God's glory is revealed either through us or in spite of us. The mission is God's mission, including the mission of "thy kingdom come." We become a part of God's mission, but it does not fall on us to "eradicate evil" or "end poverty" or "bring justice." In the words of Tyler Wigg-Stevenson, "The world is not ours to save . . . or damn. Only serve the One whose it is."[24]

Each human act of beauty, truth, and goodness has its own destiny. Just as every book has its own destiny apart from its author, so too does every act of compassion and kindness. Sometimes that destiny is immediate. But most often that destiny is delayed or detoured or distant.

Lack of Liturgical Consciousness

Another fatal flaw in the first social gospel was its lack of liturgical consciousness. Aside from Walter Rauschenbusch,[25] the liturgical life of the social gospel was weak to missing. In the early church, *leitourgia,* or "liturgy," had a double meaning: It referred both to worship and to elevating the worth of others through sacred/sacrificial ministry of service—connecting people to the transfiguring power of Jesus. The Me/We of worship cannot be separated from the Me/We of mission. Celebrating good news fuels enacting good deeds. The Lord's Table is what turns the tables on real human concerns, such as persecution, addictions, and poverty.

Social gospelers were well-meaning Christians from the full spectrum of Christianity who attempted to usher in God's kingdom on earth by shoe-horning salvation into social structures and redesigning communities to carry out the "works" of Christ's teachings. However, any attempt, on whatever end of the theological spectrum, to move Christianity toward a mere propositional matrix rather than a relational mesh is a regressive, not a progressive, act. Much of the social gospel movement collapsed into a collective soteriology, promising "salvation" to economic systems and political structures, humanity at large, but not expressly to individuals. And not by the power of Jesus but by the "power" of people. The more ethical structures they touted and "kingdom principles" they taught, the more the worm in the apple squirmed.

*Our humanity is diminished when we have no
mission bigger than ourselves.*

—Bono

A New Social Gospel

Relational Theology and Individual Responsibility

It is time for a new social gospel based not on kingdom-building but on kingdom-living, the kingdom-living of a whole Me/We relational faith. We find ourselves not in the mirror, not in the media, but in the faces of others and the figure of Christ. A human becomes human in the process of being known by other humans and by God. We become human through our relationships with God and others. In the process of becoming known by other humans and by God, we come to know ourselves.[26] In Christ, we construct a new self, which is not, paradoxically, self-constructed but divinely

10

constructed from the voice of God, speaking to the voice of self, through the voice of the neighbor, heard in the voice of creation.

The empire of Me is empty—empty of empathy for others and empty of treasures for oneself. Every Me is an integral limb of an organic We rooted in Jesus, from whom we derive our core identity. Our relationships with God and each other are intrinsic to the integrity of our identity as human beings and as collective "bodies" of Christ. Discipleship is a We garden made up of an infinite number of Me individuals. Discipleship is a story lived together, authored by God, and scripted and scribed by people who are all uniquely designed by God.

The Living Body of Christ in the World

The gospel is not a sequence of rules and acts but an organic and living Christ within the world. The social gospel was anything but organic. It was human designed and construct focused. "Let's 'save' social systems we created by incorporating 'Christian' principles, ethics, and works that we define as Christian," they said.

What's wrong with that? The social gospel model was the quintessential toolbox of an agnostic faith, one that says, "God's not powerful enough, so we'll need to 'build the kingdom' by ourselves." It says, "We can do 'Jesus' better than Jesus." It says, "We can build a better turtle." And "The most important thing about a turtle is the structure of its shell." Never mind that the shell of a turtle is attached to its body. Never mind that the shape and stamp of its shell has little to do with the animal's health or lifeline, or from whence it receives its breath. Never mind that within that superimposed new structure, a creature is still slowly dying. Never mind that no new shell in the world can save a life unless the power of Jesus has healed it and made a whole turtle whole. The health of any shell is only a reflection of the health of the living or ailing being within. The same way our skin reflects the health of our body, so our bodies of faith are only as healthy as the Spirit within.

To be healed and whole, we need to be healed mind, body, and soul by the True Healer. The same way abandoned ministries and missions reflect the health of a church and its communities, so do we need the healing power of Jesus, mind, body, and soul, to infuse life into the people within them. If the body is Spirit-less and ailing, it doesn't matter what container you put it in, it will still be ailing. Only the Living Water can spring forth from dry ground.

No matter how much we dig and construct and strategize, a well without water is no well at all; and a "house" without Jesus is no house at all. The social gospel tried to build a well without the Living Water. But you can't find water unless the Living Spring is there.

God was here, and I didn't even know it!
—Genesis 28:16 (AT) about Jacob's Ladder in a place called Bethel

---

For Jesus, salvation was not victory over one's enemies or transformation of social structures but healing of mind, body, and spirit; reclamation of relationships; and restoration to community. Social systems, institutions, and structures are human-built mechanisms. They can no more reach heaven than a rowboat can go upstream in a tsunami. Throughout social gospel history, they have been our Towers of Babel, "3-step, 5-step, 12-step programs" to kingdom-building, complete with instruction manuals and design blueprints guaranteed to work in just about every venue. Some great institutions emerged from the social gospel movement—the Salvation Army, YMCA, YWCA, hospitals, institutes, colleges, and "institutional churches." But the movement also left a world sick with despair, impinged with doubt, and a people without a Savior.

Those who are in love with community, destroy community; those who love people, build community.
—Dietrich Bonhoeffer

God's Kingship

Jesus, the Last Adam, with the First Adam's imagination of a gardener, knew the lilies of the field. But unlike the First Adam, the Last Adam also knew the lily-livered delusions of the heart, the lies of the mind, and the alluring yarns of the world.

Basileia is most often translated "kingdom," but the best translation is not "kingdom" but "kingship." The church is the body of Christ proclaiming Christ's kingship and the kingdom at hand, enacting things liturgically that are beyond doctrinal declarations or institutional establishments. *Basileia* has more to do with person than office or territory and is even more accurate as "sovereign" than "king." God isn't sovereign over a certain territory but over all of creation, which is why to speak of the head of the church and the rule of the kingdom are the same.

Christ's Sovereignty

When the language of the "kingdom" is used, there must be a constant proclamation of Christ's sovereignty, and this is the biggest reason for the failure of the social gospel movement. It tried to do kingdom without a king. It is hard for a people founded on opposition to a king to understand that wherever the king is, there is the kingdom. The kingdom is attached to the person of the king, not to a set of documents or doctrines, principles or principalities.

The social gospel had it right in that the gospel needs to be more than just a nod-to-God hour one day a week. Faith needs to bear the fruit of action within a world full of alienation, apathy, and hurt. In fact, the term *social gospel* is a pleonasm, since any gospel that is not social is not the gospel. God's covenant is with all creatures and all creation. Christ died to save not just Me but We, not just souls but the entire created world. For there to be a new heaven and a new earth, the gospel message must be social.

Like a Mustard Seed

But the gathering of diverse people into a single body is something that is God-built, not hand-made: organic, adaptive, and self-organizing, not organized, systematic, and structured. The kingdom of God is not brought about by politics or power. It is like a seed that is planted in the ground and when watered and fertilized, it bears fruit that is picked and enjoyed as a gift from the Creator. You don't so much "enter" the kingdom of God as it "enters" you. In the disciples' prayer, "Our Father," there is only one reference to human acts: "as we forgive our debtors." The slippery slopes to becoming a "works" more than "grace" and "gratitude" people are everywhere, changing acts of faith into a chase for dangling carrots, as in the social gospel message.

The word *community* has become the new Babel. We are trying to build community when we should be following Jesus wherever he takes us and allowing God to build us up into a temple in Christ's image, one that breathes Jesus. Instead of organic, kingdom communities, we have been fashioning artificial, franchised, contrived, branded "community" within our churches and within the world. It's time not to build a kingdom but to discern and to welcome the powerful presence of the King.

Perhaps all the dragons in our lives are princesses who are only waiting to see us act, just once, with beauty and courage.

—Rainer Maria Rilke, *Letters to a Young Poet*

Freely Given, Unmerited Favor

The kingdom is not something we build or create or bring about. Every time the word for *kingdom* is used in the Bible, it describes a presence we enter, a present we receive, a promise fulfilled. You enter the kingdom not as a reward for goodness or as a response to God's "justice" but as a gift of God's goodness and mercy. We enter the kingdom not because God is just but because God is merciful.

We want a self-made, proof of improved life. Jesus offers us a spanking new, Christ-made, kingdom life. Any attempt to see Jesus's understanding of the kingdom of God as a political movement, an apocalyptic regime, or a social justice program—anything other than the revelation of God with a trinitarian personality and path to the heart—is to put ideology in the place of faith.

The function of the church is not to be a political movement; the function of the church is not to be a sociological entity. The function of the church is to be the body and bride of Christ.

The function of the church is not to bring in the kingdom. The function of the church is to be the kingdom. The church doesn't just provide humanitarian help to relieve distress or change social structures but gives back to humans their dignity as children of God, to enhance and reveal their economies of grace and encounters with the living Christ. Only God's grace can absorb the pain and poison of the world. Only God's grace can defeat those fire-breathing dragons that stalk everyone's life. God's grace is like gravity—it is inescapable but not irresistible.

14

Jesus didn't define the kingdom. He didn't say what the kingdom of God "is." He said what the kingdom of God is "like." He used similitudes, metaphors, parables, stories to introduce us to God's version of kingdom. The closest he came to defining the kingdom was to say "the kingdom of God is within you" and "among you."[27] Otherwise Jesus told a bunch of "likes." In other words, he defined the kingdom in a way that led less to conclusions than to conversations, less to politics than to semiotics. We talk obliquely, because we can't talk directly. We can't look the sun in the face.

How Is a Me/We Gospel Different?

An Invitation to Live in God's "House and Garden"

A Me/We gospel can be visualized by looking at any one of the many photographs in a copy of the once popular household magazine *House and Garden*, a magazine that captures the beauty of your extended domicile, the household you care for that includes both outdoor gardens and interiors. It was a domestic magazine—and good news for those whose passion was seeing homes as extended gardens. In a way, you could say the gospel is domestic good news too. The Bible is a visual diary of God's family affairs, a family that extends throughout all creation. God's "House and Garden" consists of everything that the social gospel is not. God's "House and Garden" consists of everything God created for us to reside in. Meanwhile, we are obsessed with the dwellings we built for God to "reside in." We are an *Architectural Design* crazed people living in a "House and Garden" world designed by God.

We love being the "masters of our soul," as the poem by William Earnest Henley goes: "I am the master of my fate; / I am the captain of my soul." We love being the masters of our own vineyards. Except our vineyards look more like road construction and marble palaces than living, fruit-bearing vines and the vineyards of God's world.

It's time to reevaluate our households, to acknowledge God's domain and sovereignty over the design of our "houses." Our "households" are all part of God's garden of resurrection, a place where God is always residing. The world "and all that is in it" is God's kingdom sanctuary and estuary. Situated within are the households we build. Ideally, these are inhabited by the ongoing incarnation. They should at least be designed by God. The kingdom is not a new

15

world order we can build. The kingdom is God's garden of resurrection; it is God's *basileia*, which is designed and decorated by *oikonomia*, the household economies of Christ,[28] all of which revolve around the proper arrangement of relationships and resources. Every day we live, God consigns to us the *oikonomia* design—the improbable privilege of giving household form and expression to the rising life of the Lamb of God. Jesus never separated the divine design for the individual from the common good. The Me and the We belong together.

The story of David's desire to build God a house is one of the most incredible stories in the scriptures.[29] Both the Jerusalem temple and the Jesus temple were built on puns. Just as Jesus, who came from the "house of David," founded his temple punning the word *stone*, so Solomon's temple is founded on a pun of the word *house* (*bayit*). "The Lord will make you a house"[30] is a pun on the two meanings of the word *house*: a "dwelling place" such as a house or temple, and "a dynasty" of a people, a "house" of faith that is always under construction. We live in a dwelling place, and we are a dwelling place. You live in a house, but a house lives in you. In each of our houses there dwell many personalities, many dreams, many decorations. While building our house, a lifelong project, the house of God is also building us up as well.

In our version of God's house, there are many mansions, and many outhouses, too few lighthouses, too many haunted houses, and too many dollhouse versions of life. The challenge of life is never to retire from building and being a house of faith, never to retire to the rest home of religious belief but to keep our "Under Construction" signs and "Architect Yahweh" cornerstones up and active until we are told by God to lay down our tools. When we bluff and bully our way to building our own structures and systems apart from God's mission in the world, we find ourselves maintaining the bricks and mortar of Babel and not the "living stones" of the true temple.

End of Construction—
Thank you for your patience.
—Ruth Bell Graham's tombstone etching

In Sweden, they have a custom that when a new house is built, they fasten to its roof a small evergreen tree. When the house is finished, they decorate the tree, drape the house in lights, and throw a big party. That's what a true "memorial celebration" is supposed to be. We spend our lives being built up, and at the moment of glorification, the resurrection celebration begins!

God Makes Us a We

God's "signature" is the invisible stamp on every garden, on every household economy, on every incarnation of relationships. And while our self-made constructs are an exercise in singularity, God's signature is a creation constructed on connections.

We live in a disconnected world of Me *versus* We. The decline in our churches is not just about people rejecting church. They are rejecting commitment to anything except themselves. How did we get so disconnected, so divided, so pillared with polarizing categories of rich/poor, black/white, liberal/conservative, 99 percent/1 percent?

By thinking bricks and mechanisms and forgetting the Me and We within them, we have allowed the fissures in our houses to grow and widen. Our "houses" are in great need of healing. That healing must begin with new kinds of connectedness, or what sociologists call "third places."[31] People today congregate not on shared streets but around shared interests. But the more we congregate on shared walls, the more we yearn to congregate on shared streets and porches again.

Me Does Not Dissolve into We

God created Me to be in We relationships. God created a We world bound by a We covenant that still recognizes the Me in every person as part of God's We image.[32] Not only did we try to separate our house from our garden, but also we tried to save our houses (that's *so* Babel) instead of pointing people in the directions of Jacob's "ladders" (God's stairways to heaven—the signs of God's presence in the world), the true hope for the people within God's garden kingdom. When we see our households as staples of the garden, not as additions stapled upon it, the whole world becomes a sacred "House and Garden."

You are holding a book that sees organic staples and stairways in everything. It explores ways in which our gardens and pathways can become more beautiful, even as we recognize God's designer "handprint" upon them, and how our households can become more like our gardens, as we "tend" them and "till" them (conserve and conceive them) within God's image as reflectors of a garden lifestyle.

Christianity is not a moral theory, but a love story between
God and humanity that was consummated in Christ.

—Timothy Radcliffe, *Take the Plunge*

A Social Gospel Is a "House and Garden" Gospel

A Me/We gospel is a "House and Garden" gospel. God's kingdom is a mansion not made with hands but that is built upon God's original image (DNA), finds its identity in Jesus, and grows lavishly through a garden-style economics of organic relationships and connections. A whole Me/We gospel is not social morals cloaked as Christianity; it is not political agenda masked as religion; it is the gift of a body by the Holy Spirit to a people. The Christian life is not a code of moralisms, doctrinal creeds, or a semantic/semiotic system. It's a daily indwelling of a Jesus spirit and outcropping of a Jesus life story. You can't save a system. You can only save a people. Connectedness is the DNA (Godprint) of life. Not connective mechanisms but connective relationships. Holding hands is true community, not holding meetings or holding court.

The word *ubuntu* ("humanness") is now a cliché in South Africa. It comes from the Zulu maxim *umuntu ngumuntu ngabantu* ("a person is a person through other persons"), which affirms that my humanity is bound up with yours, that one isn't just born a human being but must become a human being, and that we live on the border between each other, between *ubu* (We) and *ntu* (Me).[33]

The intimate relationship between the Me and the We, where the We embraces all of creation, was revealed in a comment by an executive of TWA (Trans World Airlines [1925–2001]), also a passionate environmentalist and a pilot who made somewhat of a name for himself because of his skill at flying. On a solo flight over the Rocky Mountains on his way to San Francisco in July 1938, Charles Lindbergh mused about his reaction: "I owned the world that hour as I rode over it, . . . free of the earth, free of the mountains, free of the clouds—yet how inseparably I was bound to them."[34] The relationship between Me and We is a passionate affair—not just with humanity but with all of God's creation. One of the biggest problems we have today in our churches and in our world is lack of passion for Christ, for creation, for all of our relationships. And that lack of passion falls quickly into apathy and an attitude of noncaring.

Laodicea was the perfect garden city. It boasted a hot water channel from Heropolis and a cold water channel from Colossea, so that it became known for its healing mineral baths. But instead of offering two extreme water experiences, one hot and one cold, Laodicea was careless in its water program so that by the time water reached the city, it was unappealingly tepid and lukewarm. A "lukewarm" faith is what Paul criticized so ably and what still threatens to paralyze us today.

The biblical story is a haggadic pasticcio of paradoxical realities—"outside, within, above, below, before, and beyond all logical truth," as Martin Luther put it.[35] Of course, intrinsic to Judaism is debate and discourse, and Talmudic double-rings are called "haggadic antinomy." Often in the Haggadah, there is this fireworks of paradox, this both/and-ness: two texts that appear to be contradictory that are actually mutually dependent. The scientific community went mad when Werner Heisenberg suggested that one could have two mutually exclusive propositions on the same theme at the same time, and both correct. Heisenberg was not Jewish, but he almost became a victim of Nazism, because he was a defender of Einstein in particular and "Jewish physics" in general.

Christianity is a superhuman paradox whereby two opposite passions may blaze beside each other.

—G. K. Chesterton, *Orthodoxy*

Not Either/Or but Both/And

The key to the human spirit is the creative force of paradox, where the high and the low, the black and the white, the wise and the foolish, the *kenosis* and the *plerosis*, the saint and the sinner not only coexist but feed off each other. This is how the gospel can be fresh though ancient, familiar yet new. But the paradoxy of faith is the play of a paradoxical dynamic. It is not

19

a paradoxical dialectic that is in need of the transcendence of opposites in some resolution. Hypocrisy, even heresy, is to ignore or deny the play of one or the other legs of the dynamic. Orthodoxy is paradoxy, even the Ultimate Paradox: God became what God is not—one of us, flesh and blood, God incarnated in life and letter, stable and table.

It is no wonder that the Ultimate Paradox—the Human One and the Divine One, David's Son and David's Lord, Lamb, and Lion—was a master of paradox and punning. As we have seen, when Jesus names Peter to build his second temple, he playfully puns with his name. Jesus tells Peter that he is a *petros* (Me stone), and upon this *petra* (We bedrock) "I will build my church." The Me is built upon the We and becomes one whole. Paradox gives Christianity its rich and playful intellectual life.[36]

A Me/We gospel embraces the unity of paradoxy, embraces the beauty in difference and the relationality of everything and everyone in God's vast created world.

The navel is a powerful image for paradox: It is a knot that both binds the body and marks its point of severance. The navel of Christianity is the Me/We gospel. It is both a point of birthing and a point of identity.

Me/We: Birthing a New Creation

This book is about garden-fresh faith and the willingness to give God's power back to God. Going "back to the start" and rethinking a Genesis theology that puts God back in charge, Me/We offers up new perspectives on community, church, world, and relationships that eliminate divisions and dichotomies and embrace relational unity. It looks at how returning to our "place" in the garden can give us new looks at how we see the world and how we see each other, how we assess our lives and how we build an "economy" of hope in a Babel-built community.

From the birthing of creation to a garden-style economy, come walk with me through God's version of "House and Garden." Because, as the early Hebrews knew, "everything you wanted to know about God, you've already learned in Genesis."

"Only Connect": The Gospel of Me and We

A Biblical Story

---

*Everything you need to know about God,
you've already learned in Genesis.*

It is no historical happenstance that individualism and depression (melancholia) developed simultaneously in Western culture from 1600 upwards. This chapter explores the nature of de-selfing in a selfie culture. A super-Me, wee-We society drags everything before the tribunal of the sacred self, where a form of individual infallibility arbiters all of life with almost total and absolute authority. You can live life "my way," as in "I Did It My Way." You can live life "our way," as in "I Did It Our Way." Or you can live life "the Way," as in "I Did It the Way of Jesus—the Way, the Truth, and the Life." The first is to live individually as Me. The second is to live collaboratively as We. The third is to live christologically as Me/We, where the pursuit of Me integrity within a We community requires cultivating a Christ identity.

Me and We: The Central Question

"Only Connect." These two words from E. M. Forster's *Howard's End* (1910) have resonated powerfully over the years because of their oxymoronic ring: "Only" and "Connect." The "only" suggests Me. The "connect" suggests We. Put the two words together as one and there is true being. Me + We = Be.

The relationship between those two words, *me* and *we*, our apart-ness and our part-ness, our separateness and our connection, is arguably the central question of human life. Each human being is a separate life but in the same ecosystem. Each human being is an original, one-of-a-kind wave but in the same ocean. It is a basic human axiom that every human being is different from everyone else and the same as everyone else. We may talk the game of the singular ("early Christianity," "ancient Rome," "first world," "late modern"), but nothing forms a single entity. The One and the Many, the individual and the communal, are inseparable.

The way that word *love* connects the Me and the We, the personal and the communal, is perhaps the organizing obsession of Christianity. *Love* is a relational word, by definition. What better way to convey the truth of a God who is Love than by a trinitarian understanding of God as Love, Lover, and Loved?

Jesus wants each of us to be an original expression of reality, not just a replication of reality; a manifestation of truth, not just a mimicker of truth. The affirmation of the individual (Me) in the face of depersonalizing crowds and uniformed masses that would drive out great personalities is one of the major plotlines of the story of salvation. Your odd features, those things that make you uniquely you, are God's way of manifesting the beauty of the divine.

But the key to a singular life is connectedness. The union of all is built on the uniqueness of each, and the uniqueness of each person is in the ubiquity of connections. Is God so unimaginative that we are all patterned in the same mold? Does Jesus produce clones or characters? Each person is a place of inexhaustible mystery. Or as Augustine put it, "[Each person] is a great deep." I need a Savior—to save me from myself, so I can be myself and be more than myself.

There is an old story about a clever spider who managed to construct a magnificent, beautifully patterned web, an elegant work of art. The web was so marvelously constructed that spiders from all over the area came to gaze at it. The web was so symmetrical that if one could have folded it over at the middle, the two sides would fit exactly over each other. The match was perfect.

The spider, of course, was very pleased with its creation. One morning it made its usual inspection of the web, tightening up a knot here and loosening another thread there. All seemed to be in order until the spider saw a thread it didn't recognize. What could it be? Where did it come from? It was very long, and it didn't seem to fit. It broke the symmetry. "Who needs it?" the spider thought. And so, the creature bit it off, whereupon the entire web collapsed and the spider had a big fall.

The one essential thread that held the beautifully patterned web together, the thread on which the spider's whole world depended, had been broken: disconnected. The great heresy of the mind is the illusion of separateness: the notion that I am here, and you are out there. We're only ourselves when we're connected. Being alive is a shared experience. To get a life, you've got to get a connective life. Borrowing a lyric from the English progressive rock band Marillion in "Jigsaw," "We are Siamese children related by the heart."

On my honor
I will do my best
to help myself
and cheat the rest.

—Anonymous

"You are your own," "You are what you own," and "You're on your own" are the first three principles of hell.

Playwright/screenwriter John L. Balderson (1889–1954), known for his horror scripts, wrote about a man who dies and passes into the next world. When he opens his eyes, he sees laid out before him more beauty and luxury than he ever dreamed possible, more than he ever dared hope for. Every wish is granted instantly. At the slightest whim, an attendant appears to see that his every desire is immediately fulfilled.

After a time, the man grows bored and restless. "If only, just once, there were some push-back, some feedback, even a refusal." Finally, the monotony becomes unbearable, and he summons the attendant. "I want something that I can't have. I want you to tell me 'no.'"

"Sorry," the attendant replies, "that's the one wish we cannot grant here."

"Very well, then," the man says. "I want out. Let me out of here. I would rather be in hell."

Whereupon the attendant asks, "And where do you think you are, sir?"

The heaven's truth?

When Jesus is asked about what is owed to the empire, he answers by talking about what is owed to God. "Give to the state what belongs to it," he says. If the money belongs to the state, give it that money. It bears the "image" of the state, doesn't it?[1] But *you* belong to God. You bear the image of God. The trick, of course, of the answer lies in that not only do we belong to God but that everything connected to us in our daily lives and in the created world, both "House and Garden," belong to God. What we believe we "own" is a grand illusion. And the "images" we create for ourselves are equally delusional. In his clever answer, Jesus instructed that God is the creator of everything. God's "image" is embedded, inscribed, intrinsically engraved on all that we think we own, and God's signature trumps everything in the end.

Jesus's message to us in everything is:

1. "You are *not* your own";[2] "It is He who has made us, and not we ourselves."[3]

2. You own nothing. "Every good gift is from God."[4] "All you own you owe."[5]

3. "I will never leave you nor forsake you."[6]

A Me/We world is a world that acknowledges both the sovereignty of God as the Master Gardener and the connectedness of all created things. A Me/We church is a garden-style community.

Jesus's Team: A Community of Interdependent Individuals

We all live a double life. Or more theologically, as Aelred of Rivaulx would have it, Christians live a third life: "Here we are, thou and I, and I hope that between us Christ is a third."[7] The paradox of Me/We is not resolved in mediation or in resolution or in equilibrium but in the dialectic dynamic of the relationship between the two, a syncopated, punctuated "between-ness" that issues in a third reality.[8]

A Me/We gospel insists on living on a two-way street: Faith is communal, but faith is individual. Individualism as an ideology or a philosophy is bad. Individuality is good. In a Me/We gospel, we proclaim our individuality and our interdependence at the same time. The pioneer Dutch entomologist

Jan Swammerdam (1637–1680) looked at an ant colony and saw an idyllic Christian existence: "Love and unanimity, more powerful than punishment or death itself, preside there, and all live together in the same manner as the primitive Christians anciently did, who were connected by fraternal love, and had all things in common."[9]

An ant colony was not Jesus's idea of paradise. Jesus does not subordinate the individual to the community nor the community to the individual. Rather, Jesus understood every community to be comprised of uniquely important individuals.

The Spirit is given to each one who receives Him as if
He were the possession of that person alone.

—Saint Basil the Great

Following Jesus requires Me/We team play. At school, the reward goes to the child who first raises a hand and shouts out the answer. At the Jesus school of discipleship, true victory belongs to God-empowered individuals with the freedom to live together in harmony.[10] Or as our ancestors put it, *unus christianus, nullus christianus*—a lone Christian is no Christian. We will stand before God as one, not as many.[11] We can know together what we can never know alone. But some things we can only know alone. Some people think of humans the way one house guest said of a tree I was showing him: "If you've seen one tree, you've seen them all. A tree is a tree." A tree is not a tree, and a person is not a person. A person is a particular person in a particular place with a particular bent and elements of character and carriage particular only to him or her.

The strength of the team is each individual member.
The strength of each member is the team.

—Phil Jackson

Jesus lived his whole life in the extremes of solitude and multitude: (1) surrounded by people and studied by disciples; (2) in prayerful solitude or the solicitude of a few close friends. The Me/We rhythms of multitude and solitude, which structured Jesus's life, can be likened to an accordion.[12] If we are always together or always apart, there is no music. It is the moving in and out of separateness and togetherness that makes the music.

Togetherness depends on authentic aloneness.
—Rabbi Joshua Boettiger

Those annoying, endless lists of everlasting *begats* that slow down the biblical narrative? Each list of names is a protest against all totalitarian attempts to efface individuality, and each list of names is a protest against all autonomous arrogance that denies covenant connectedness.[13] Community without individuality becomes repressive; individuality without community becomes anarchic.

Rabbi Zusia of Hanipol (1718–1800), the Hasidic luminary and favorite of Martin Buber, came to his followers one day, his eyes

> red with tears and his face pale with fear. He told them that he had learned the question God would ask him in the coming world about his life. His followers were puzzled. "Zusia," they said, "you are pious, scholarly, and humble. What question about your life could be so terrifying that you would be frightened to answer it?" Zusia answered, "I have learned that God will not ask me, 'Why were you not Moses, leading your people out of slavery?' Nor will he ask me, 'Why were you not Joshua, leading your people into the Promised Land?' God will say to me, 'Zusia, there was only one thing that no power of heaven or earth could have prevented you from becoming: Why were you not Zusia?'"[14]

Individual lives intersect to connect and influence each other, an idea that is conveyed in Paul's breathtaking "body" metaphor for the resurrection presence of Christ. We aren't the whole body, but we are a part of the whole body, and the whole body is present in each part.

Entangled by Language

Both these words *individual* and *communal*, or *individuality* and *community*, are some of the most problematic words in circulation today. John

Locke's *Essay Concerning Human Understanding* (1690), one of the most influential essays in history, is a centerpiece for the equation of modernity with individualism. Locke's essay, which had a profound influence on John Wesley, defined the self in a way that didn't help matters much:

> Every one is to himself that which he calls *self*. . . . For . . . consciousness always accompanies thinking, and 'tis that, that makes everyone to be, what he calls *self*; and thereby distinguishes himself from other thinking beings. . . . It is by the consciousness it has of its previous Thoughts and Actions, that it is *self* to it *self* now, and so will be the same *self* as far as the same consciousness can extend to actions past or to come.[15]

The word *individual* is problematic, because the concept that we act independently of one another has no basis in life. You and I are made up of relationships—organ systems (twelve of them) in relationship, and creatures in relationship. How important are relationships to the story of the human species? Augustine suggested that Adam "fell" because he would rather die outside the garden with Eve than live forever in paradise without her. He could not bear to be without her, so the husband submitted to the wife.[16] Adam sinned with his eyes wide open.

Where the Notion of the Individual Came From

But first, where did we get the notion of *individual* from? The concept of the individual as we know it today is a gift of Jesus to the history of the world. For Jesus, holiness is not an arrogation of superiority but an avowal of the holiness of every human. God cares for the one . . . one coin, one sheep, one son, one sinner who repents. God knows every sparrow that falls,[17] keeps a record of your every tear,[18] and numbers every hair on your head.[19] Jesus's concern for the individual is striking. For Jesus, everyone counts, including all no-accounts. The image of heaven is one where We praise and worship God but where each Me has our individual name written on our forehead, as well as a secret name given only to us written on a white stone we hold in our hands.

Whoever cannot be alone should beware of community. Whoever cannot stand being in community should beware of being alone.

—Dietrich Bonhoeffer, *Life Together*

Jesus placed us under an "equal to it" obligation to love our neighbors and care for them at least nineteen centuries before anyone thought of doing so through the medium of a nation-state: "Love the Lord Your God, *and equal to it*, Love Your Neighbor As yourself."[20] Once individual moral agency entered the human consciousness, it altered our symbolic universe forever and revolutionized all relationships. The Human One's call to be human is the call of the incarnation to be flesh to our neighbor; to be blood to our needy; to be bread to our hungry and hurting.

Followers of Jesus, first and most notably Paul, virtually invented individual conscience, opposed hierarchy, believed in the equality of souls, and were proponents of human rights. Notions of equal human liberty were born in early Christian apologetics, and it was the Middle Ages followed by the Protestant Reformation that saw the discovery of the individual as we know it today, not the Italian Renaissance or Enlightenment culture.[21] Equality of individuals, or the notion that every person (male/female, Jew/Gentile, father/son, master/slave) is endowed with equal human status, is a "child of Christianity."[22] It is only in the Christian tradition that you can find someone like Russian philosopher Nikolai Berdyaev (1874–1948), who argued that every human soul has more meaning and value than the whole of history with its empires, wars, and revolutions.

Where Our Notion of Community Came From

In a world that had no concept of free will or the "individual" separate from the family or the nation, Christianity revolutionized the world with its concept of human equality and free will. Created equal under God, as moral agents with free will, Christians created a revolution in moral sensibilities that made "equal individuals" the overarching cultural principle in the West, detonating the ancient order of pedigree and privilege. Church fathers were the protagonists of egalitarianism and developed some of the radical social implications of egalitarianism that we take for granted today, including the notion of the community as a free association of the wills of morally equal individuals, or what Paul reframes more organically as the "body of Christ." Even the very concept of secularism, which is falsely defined as the absence of religion rather than the differentiation of the temporal and the eternal, is a derivative of Christianity's revolt from antiquity's fusion of the religious with the social and political. To remove Christianity from the public square in favor of enshrining the liberal values of "secularism" is more complex and muddled than mere "disestablishment," since those very "liberal values" so touted by "secularism" are rooted in Christianity. Indeed the very ground on which we walk, even for atheists, is the ground that grew Christian faith, the ground that grew Western culture itself, the ground that hoisted the very goalposts of liberal values themselves.

"Borged" by TGIF?

The postmodern osmosis of the individual and the communal is shaving the edges off the Me and swallowing it up in the We. We are being "Borged" by consumer, celebrity culture, even as we sacrilize the self, though not a self of our own making or God's making. I grew up on *Star Trek*, where my favorite villain was the Borg, the collective consciousness that assimilates personal identity into its beehive collectivity, and collapses the Me into the We.

In a digital TGIF (Twitter, Google, Instagram, Facebook) culture, we stand out in cyberspace by "sounding more like everyone else than anyone else is able to sound like everyone else."[23] The spirit of sameness spreading through the church and culture makes everything smaller and everyone shallower. The spirit of "getting along" fetters freedom and eradicates individuality. In a world where "individual" is increasingly suspect and even a bad word, in a world reigned by "sensitivity" czars who rain their wrath on any violations of conformity, Christianity is moving toward more cosmic and corporate We spiritualities. The church used to tell you what to think, and burnt you if you didn't think it. It hasn't changed much. Now it's a faceless, robeless political correctitude that tells you what to think, and "burns" you if you don't.

TGIF culture is a movement away from Me to We, that is, except in formerly communist, totalitarian countries (e.g., Poland), where Christians are sensitive to any moves that wipe out the individual, immanent Me aspects of faith.[24] Why did the military and diplomatic apparatus of the fascist regime of Mussolini rescue the Jews? In Italy, the Jews were seen as individual human beings. In Germany, where Hegelian thinking collectivized everything (even people) into abstract categories, Jews were seen as *das Judentum*, a dehumanized collectivity, and increasingly blamed for all the ills of German society long before Hitler arrived on the scene.[25]

Faith Is Not Do-It-Yourself

You cannot pray the Lord's Prayer and pray for yourself, or only for yourself. Faith is not a make-it-up-for-yourself, personal do-it-yourself life project. Faith is a personal life practice, conducted in community. The self is social, semantic, and semiotic. Self-giving (We) is the noblest form of self-fulfillment (Me).

This is the manner of noble souls: they do not want to have anything for nothing; least of all, life. Whoever is of the mob wants to live for nothing; we others, however, to whom life gave itself, we always think about what we might best give in return. . . . One should not wish to enjoy where one does not give joy.

—Friedrich Nietzsche, *Thus Spoke Zarathustra*

In fact, the community comes first, before the individual.[26] A person is born into community. No one begins life entirely from scratch. We are born into a We, a tribe and tradition whose language we learn before we bend that We into a Me direction and separate ourselves from other persons. Born from the side of Christ, the church is older than the writings of Paul and Mark, Luke, John, and Matthew. In a sense, the church wrote the New Testament. Criticize the church, but you're criticizing Jesus's bride. And it's our family. Until we can say "This is my body," and it be like pulling a picture out of a wallet and saying "this is my family," we aren't getting Jesus.

We demand personal freedom. But once we get it, how do we first exercise our hard-won personal freedom? We join a group, cause, theory. We humans are such social creatures, such pack animals; we live such lemming lives. The whole of "celebrity culture" can be seen as a narrative vehicle for people who are looking for a rewrite, for potted narratives, or a copy editor (internal or external) to give them a bigger and better storyline. We are so afraid of living our own story that we give up our freedom of authorship, and authority over our lives, to others. The only story you can trust with your life is the Jesus story.

When Me Is Cut Off from We

When the Me is emancipated from the We (clan, church, guild, and other local forms of community), as happened in modernity, there is an attraction to mass movements, nationalist illusions, personality cults—a.k.a. fascism, communism, totalitarianism. In other words, hyper-Me produces its own hyper-We—conformism, submission, and control.[27]

A community mind can quickly become a pack mentality, especially when it loses the mind of Christ. When there's a pile-on, no matter how horrid the offense or egregious the cause, I get nervous. Pile-ons become packs, and nothing is worse than the mass madness of community sadism, a We gone feral. Charles Mackay, Charles Dickens's friend and the author of *Extraordinary Popular Delusions and the Madness of Crowds* (1841), spent a whole book demonstrating how "men, it has been well said, think in herds; it will be seen that they go mad in herds, while they only recover their senses slowly, and one by one."

One mighty deed alone was sufficient for our God—to bring freedom to the human person.

—Tertullian, *Adversus Marcionem*

Me Fits into We

Following Jesus is not a benign dedication but a commitment to a body (body of Christ) to whom one has already become a life member when baptized. This commitment to fitting together as one body is at base an artistic one. Our very word *art* comes from an Indo-European root meaning "to fit together," as does the root of the word *religion* from *religare*, which means "fit together." An artisanal expression of the gospel is another way of talking about the incarnation, which places artisanship and craftsmanship at the heart of living the gospel in the world.

One of my "interactives" that animates the nature of a body's connectedness is to get twelve people to stand in two parallel lines. I then ask them to link hands. Normally they will hold hands with the person on either side of them. Now I ask them to raise their arms in the air and make a roof. Isn't that another way to link hands? But this time, I show them how easy it is to knock the roof down. I ask them one more time—link hands. But this time reach across and form four-way arches. I then show them how strong these rafters are—so strong a grown person can easily hang from them (someone always volunteers). I finish the interactive by

31

revealing to them that they have just built the cantilevered arches of the medieval cathedral.

The very design of cathedrals is connective, just as the very design of life is connective. But I didn't learn this from medieval cathedrals. I learned how relationships rule from my kids. Thane, Soren, and Egil have a favorite place in the whole world: Taylors of Tabernacle Camp Meeting. One of two thousand continuous camp meetings still in existence today, Taylors of Tabernacle takes place every year in the hottest time of the year (July), in the midst of an isolated cornfield, in the middle of rural Tennessee (ten miles outside Brownsville). There is barely running water, much less electronics or any of the amenities of home. But true reality, no matter how hot and sweaty, grimy and disquieting, always trumps virtual reality. There is no substitute for the real thing—and the real thing is relationships and community, kith and kin. Our problem is that we so seldom give our kids the real thing, only artificials and facsimiles.

Sociologists tell us that membership in a human community is the most important social good.[28] But it makes all the difference in the world what kind of community we are talking about. Baby-boomers think they're living in community when they're living in condominiums or gated communities. Sadly, my generation is responsible for turning the church into communities of convenience and comfort, not commitment and mission. The average New Yorker meets as many people in one week as a first-century person would have met in a lifetime. Yet the number of true meetings among those "meets" is virtually nonexistent. Contrast that with the average Hebrew household of the first century, which numbered anywhere from forty to one hundred people.[29] These families were like small villages made up of several adjacent buildings. The people you saw outside your small village were mostly kith and kin.

Biblical We-ness

Perhaps the most sophisticated reflection on the nature of true connectedness is known as "Catholic Social Teaching." Centuries of theological reflection and ecclesial conversation have distilled the essence of biblical We-ness into a trinity of S's: solidarity, subsidiarity, and sustainability.

Solidarity

Art in medieval churches used to be seen as owned by every member of the community. When a church got a new work of art, it was celebrated by the whole community. Then art moved into our homes and museums, privatizing and personalizing both art and artist, and removing them both from the public square.

The solidarity of the body is a solidarity of the wounded whole, or more precisely, a solidarity that "makes the wounded whole," as the old "Balm in Gilead" spiritual puts it. There is an ancient African proverb that expresses the basis of this "wounded whole" solidarity: "When a thorn is stuck in the toe, the whole body stoops to pick it out." The essence of solidarity is the willingness to suspend personal self-interest for the sake of a community. That's why a connective sense is different from a communal sense: There can be no true Me wisdom or understanding without communal We connections.

What makes a great church? Not its size or buildings or heritage or preacher or quality of its membership. What makes a church truly great is the real-as-life presence of Christ and its faithful living of the story. What gave rise to Christianity? It was not the disciples' superior moral precepts. It was their proclamation that Jesus rose from the dead and was in some form still alive in them. This is what birthed the church, and what still holds a Jesus community together. Not rules. Not fear. Not causes. Not programs. Grace—the free gift of love and mercy that makes us participants in the divine nature—is the glue of Me/We solidarity.

John Wesley led the Wesleyan revival at a time when his culture was in the midst of one of the worst crime waves in English history. Some 80,000 sailors and soldiers had been demobilized following the Peace of Aix-la-Chapelle (1748), which stopped for a time the warfare between England and France. But Wesley addressed this issue of sailors and soldiers continuing their violence at home, not by proclaiming "Thou shalt not steal" but by declaring "Jesus is Lord."

Both George Orwell and G. K. Chesterton had a common foe: the highbrow intellectual. Both had a common cause: the English common man. But both railed against the other, especially Orwell against Chesterton, because they refused to sit down together and forgive each other for what each said about the other. The grace of a living God, not the rule-ridden, fear-riddled ropes and tropes that fasten down and tighten up the communities of the world, is the basis of community solidarity. To accept another in grace means we can have fellowship with difference not just sameness. The singular mind of Christ is what guides the multijointed body into an organic, changing, diverse body with God's signature engraved in every cell.

A Me/We whole gospel rejects the solidarity of sameness for the solidarity of interdependence and difference. A Me/We Jesus community is built less around common values and "correct principles" than around differences and conflicts.[30] Stories are heard out and prized, even when they sound strange and alien,[31] even when they are from your "enemies." Every year I live on an island the more this old saying becomes real: "An enemy on an island, as in a prison, is an enemy forever and deeply."[32] Since planet earth is an island, it behooves us not to have enemies. Why then do so many choose to make whole *generations*, whole *cultures*, whole *people-groups* their enemy-islands? Even when your enemies back themselves into a corner, you look the other way until they can get out, then act as if nothing happened. Solidarity means we each need basket loads, if not barrelfuls, of grace.

In the first century, shepherds had joined sailors, camel drivers, butchers, and others as members of a despised occupational group. This is why Luke has shepherds visit the infant Jesus: He is kick-starting his recurring theme of how Jesus defies all norms and goes to the outcasts and those on the margins of society.

But Jesus didn't consider anyone "other." He didn't reach out to the outcasts and lepers as others but as brothers and sisters. Jesus never acknowledged a category of Other. Creating a category of Other puts distance between us and others, between us and Jesus, when Jesus wants solidarity: "inasmuch as you did it to the least of these, you did it to me."[33] To even admit the categories of "self" and "other" is not to understand Jesus, for whom there are no "others," only "one anothers." How many Christians are full of activity, full of good deeds, buzzing beehives of virtuosity—the sort of person who "lives for others—you can tell the others by their hunted expression" (as C. S. Lewis[34] put it). Christianity is more than a chicken-broth of brotherly/sisterly love, but it is not less than that.

If you cross over the sea,
Instead of over the way,
[you may end by]
looking on We
As only a sort of They.

—Rudyard Kipling, "We and They"

34

In truth, people don't hate the "other" so much as they hate the ones they know. When Jesus's own family turns on him, and he asks the question "Who are my mother and my brothers?" he does not answer the question with an individualism that justified "going it alone." Rather, he created a new family solidarity to replace the old one, a disciple band where the ties were forged with the blood of obedience rather than the blood of clan.[35]

A test of true solidarity: When you don't get your own way, can you maintain unity of Spirit—no division, no discord, only magnanimity and grace? For Thomas Aquinas, the surest test of the Spirit is a simple one: Does it draw us closer together into unity? Of course, Jesus said it first in John 17, and Paul said it second in 1 Corinthians 13. A Spirit-whisperer is someone who draws a disciple deeper into the mutual and reciprocal love of the Father and the Son.

Solidarity means you keep in check the four distancing strategies that reinforce inhumanity and get people to see certain people as "others" (e.g., for Christians Muslims became "Turks" and for Muslims Serbs became "Chetniks"). The first is minimizing—"it's not as bad as people say." The second is scapegoating—"others are more responsible than me." The third is absenteeism—"I wasn't there when it happened." The fourth is equalizing—"the other side is just as bad." Strategies of solidarity create healing and wholeness and shun platforms of dichotomy and dualism.

Perhaps the most persistent conundrum of solidarity is this: How do we reconcile equality and diversity? Sometimes called the "equality-difference paradox,"[36] we hold the "paradoxical idea that society should celebrate difference with the idea that this difference doesn't really matter," as social psychologist Hazel Markus puts it. We celebrate racial and ethnic diversity but fall silent on cultural/lifestyle diversity.

Michael Jindra is one of the few scholars courageous enough to address the sensitive overlapping of culture and poverty.[37] We legislate equality through building codes, and all sorts of regulations and laws that cover housing, street vending, as well as untold aesthetics (sounds, smells, yard appearances). As if that isn't enough, gated communities have their own "covenants" that ensure obedience to equalizing codicils and protocols.

Solidarity that means equality of results eliminates diversity. Solidarity that means equality of respect preserves diversity.[38] Of course, structural forces and agency interact with culture to shape those choices. But in some ways, equality and diversity inevitably exist in uneasy and sometimes inverse relationships. The hard truth is that to enforce economic equality is to jeopardize and de-incentivize genuine cultural diversity.

Deliberate lifestyle choices and philosophical differences in how the "good life" can be defined play significant roles in increasing inequality. Is a life on the economic margins a deviant lifestyle, a problem to be solved? What if it's a deliberate and preferred way of life?

I live on an island rich in extremes. Orcas Island abounds in "downshifters"—agrarians, grungies, unrepentant hippies and other fossils from the 1960s, "new agers" attracted to the "energy vortex," environmental fundamentalists, bohemians, and "edgeworkers," who eke out a living from the margins of the local economy. What ties all the downshifters together is that they prize leisure and conviviality to labor and economic gain. Then there are the overachievers who are super-competitive and less convivial, some of whom commute daily or weekly to Seattle and Los Angeles. And this does not begin to mention the retirees, the professionals, and the blue-collars, with their diversity of lifestyles, not all of whom are focused on wealth accumulation and indeed some of whom sacrifice wealth and work to freedom and relationships.

To preserve diverse lifestyles is to foster inequality and to put equality and diversity in tension. Not all stratification is bad. Not all people aspire to the same ladder-climbing mode of life. Not all inequality is bad, and may actually reflect something good. Inequality may reflect a society's choice of increasing lifestyle diversity, anti-materialist priorities by certain groups, tolerance for those who opt out of bourgeois standards of success and middle-class-respectability, and an embrace of "the simple life." After all, Amish live well below poverty levels but enjoy immense wealth in life.

You have made them equal to us.
—Matthew 20:12b NRSV

Today, an equal sign is the new version of the plus or thumbs-up sign. So it is hard for us to hear that, in some ways, inequality can be good and equality bad. Equality promotes mediocrity as well as collegiality, just as inequality promotes excellence as well as social dislocation. The exercise of our productive capabilities is a part of what it means to be human, and to go through life in neutral is a part of what it means to be antihuman.

We are all born equal in our humanness. We are all born, live, and die equal before God. But we are not all equally born.[39] God's gifts are not universally distributed. God is no egalitarian.

Some people were born with talents and gifts that I can only envy, and some people were born to parents that I can only pity. Not all preachers are equally worth hearing, but all have an equal calling. Relationships are never equal—we are beautifully and individually and uniquely made. Solidarity means you are free to be different, and the culture does not enforce conformity or uniformity.

Not all members of the body are equal, but all are equal members. No one can be of more value than another. One can be of more service, yes. But not more value. Equality and inequality can coexist and even thrive on one another.[40]

For some people, the most important thing about life is "What's your salary?" or "What's your religion?" For Jesus, the most important thing about life is "Whom do you love?" That question can be answered in a variety of ways, and with a multiplicity of lifestyles.

Trinitatrian solidarity is based on three unique kinds of relationships foreign to the culture: *perichōrēsis*, *kenōsis*, and *agapē*.[41] *Agapē* means relationships based on sacrificial love. *Perichōrēsis* means the unity found in diversity, that one is distinguished from one another by unifying with each other. *Kenōsis* means that you lose yourself in order to find yourself; you empty yourself (*kenōsis*) to be filled (*plērōsis*). The First Adam strived to become equal to God. The Last Adam emptied himself of the glory that was his by right. Jesus became humble and obedient, even to death on the cross.

Subsidiarity

If solidarity is "we're all in this together," subsidiarity is "primary is most primal," and "elementary is most elemental." The best, most revealing view of any society is from the bottom, just as the most effective way of solving problems is from the bottom up, not the top down. Subsidiarity and solidarity are Siamese twins. A Me/We gospel brings solidarity and subsidiarity to live together in harmony.

Subsidiarity is an organizing principle that privileges decentralized modes of decision-making and design. It makes the "big" subsidiary to the smallest and the lowest. Every task should be executed at the most local level and closest distance possible.[42] Throughout history subsidiarity has fueled voluntary associations, base communities, family life, and private initiatives on the public square.

The old social gospel sought solutions in political and economic means, which have proved too often to be dead ends. The new social gospel turns to local neighborhoods and parish communities to make changes and contributions. The new social gospel particularizes in order to universalize. It turns the face of Jesus in a community outward, and lives the gospel in whatever world it finds itself in, whether that gospel be in Ninevah, Gomorrah, Issaquah, or Omaha.

Why did Noah not protest when God said God was going to destroy the world? The rabbis had various explanations: He was too pious to protest; he was too obedient; he was too fed up with people. But the rabbinic explanation I like the best was that Noah was a theologian, and he was too preoccupied with his reading and writing. We can love everyone in general so much, we do not deign to stoop to the particulars. You can be for everything and nothing at the same time. From the cosmic to the quotidian, universal to the provincial, we must parochialize the faith at the same time we globalize it. G. K. Chesterton believed that "the man who lives in a small community lives in a much larger world."[43]

Christ is God's "place." The church in its personal and communal form is Christ's "place." The Me/We social gospel pins the tale to the place; it pins the tale on the adjoining donut shop. True solidarity and subsidiarity captures the essence of a place. Just as the taste of every food reflects the sun, rain, wind, and minerals in the soil where it grew, so good living and good dying reflects the myriad tastes of the planet.

To be a citizen of God's kingdom doesn't annul your global citizenry but reframes your status as a citizen of humanity and a citizen of your neighborhood and nation. Problems like poverty, climate change, and consumerism are becoming at the same time more global and more local (i.e., less national). The church must learn to interact in the public arena, both in the local town square and in the global village square. Neither "privatization nor privilege"[44] are appropriate public square strategies for Christianity. The public square is best entrusted to neutral space, not secular space or sacred space but neutral space. A public square is not the place for "conviction politics"[45] but for civilized conversations and healing resolutions of the clash and conflict of irreconcilable convictions.[46]

A truly prophetic public voice for the church does not put the interests of Christians first but the common good first. Self-interest takes a back seat to human interest and the whole human community. A Christian should make the human case and not the "case for Christ" in the public space and in the bar of public opinion. In other words, we should be more morally and intellectually persuasive than anyone else about the nature of human values and the best prospects for the public good. Not the church's good but the public good.

It is not true that "There is no right or wrong; there is only tolerance of each other's opinions." But while there is right and wrong, Christians do not need to find themselves on the "correct" side on every issue in the public square. Furthermore, to call someone a racist or a sexist when things don't go your way—these are detonator words, releasing explosions of emotions inside everyone and militarizing the public square. Their use obviates the possibility of constructive argument. It's like calling someone evil. What do you say when someone calls you evil? Our words in the public square should be a balm in the midst of crisis, not embalm the crisis in toxic infusions of accusatory and inflammatory magniloquence.

Civility even to enemies is the glue that keeps the public square public and safe for debate. Here is what I call the Increase Mather Principle of the Public Square, as first enunciated in 1690: "It were better that ten thousand witches should escape, than that one innocent person should be condemned."

Wouldn't it be nice to live together,
In the kind of world where we'd belong?

—The Beach Boys, "Wouldn't It Be Nice"

Sustainability

If you travel from one global conference to another—most famously Davos (Switzerland) but also Wilton Park, Aspen, Valdai, Doha, Shangri-La—you will hear this word more perhaps than any other. Since 2001 there has been a fight between Davos and Porto Alegre, the twin cities of globalization. The Swiss resort of Davos is where the movers and shakers of the World

Economic Forum meet to discuss globalization. The subtropical Brazilian city of Porto Alegre is where the antiglobalization movement meets and opposes capitalist globalization. But whether you are in Davos or Porto Alegre, the word on everyone's lips is *sustainability*. It is seen as the business issue of the millennium.

But sustainability does not just equal the environment. It encompasses the health and endurance of many corners of "the Commons" as well as environmental ones. A whole Me/We gospel understanding of success is not opposed to technological progress, economic growth, efficiency, and productivity, which have been present since the beginning of time.[47] But it does ask the biting question, How much of the human spirit we are willing to sacrifice for productivity, efficiency, and prosperity? How many people are we willing to sacrifice for success? Are we sensitive to what Wendell Berry meant when he warned how growth is inescapably shrinking us?[48]

Fred D'Aguiar's "Ballad of the Throwaway People" has this:

We are the throwaway people
The problem that won't go away people.[49]

Something is really wrong with this world of ours—where ship captains get off sinking ships on the first lifeboats, where moms escape house fires and let the kids burn up. Even the musicians stayed on the *Titanic*. A culture of celebrity has replaced a culture of character. In a world of moral sleepwalking and moral dementia, where too many people have no morals but a lot of scruples and a lot more sensitivities, it is important to state that we do not live in a value-free universe. The very people who attack the "intolerance" of orthodox faith praise cultural pluralism and moral relativism with doxological zeal. Any deviation from this reigning "orthodoxy" is a "difference" not to be accommodated or celebrated.

But morality is not mere projections from our subjective preferences, or a function of a montage of urges we've inherited from some evolutionary past. The existence of cultural variation in itself does not establish the moral roulette of moral relativity. There are absolute human values that transcend and sustain cultures and command universal allegiance. You can't topple the Taliban with relativism. If you think "what's true for you is true, and what's true for me is true," then what's true for the Taliban is true, so leave them alone. And let them oppress women and violate children. Oh, you mean that's wrong? You mean that what they're doing may not be good, true, and beautiful? You mean that you really can distinguish between what is helpful and hurtful, what is pleasure and pain, and that hostility to strangers is not a virtue but kindness is?

We need morality not so much to counter evil as to counter indifference.

—Avishai Margalit, *The Ethics of Memory*

That said, the whole gospel of a Me/We faith is more than a morality, and Christianity is decidedly not a moralism. Even the Beatitudes is more a storyline of positive attitudes than prescribed ethical actions. There is no such thing as a "biblical morality," and even if there were, no one in history has been able to determine precisely what that is. Every "Christian" morality is replicated in other faith traditions, with little uniqueness to Christianity. The collapse of denominational (a.k.a. mainline) Protestantism can be attributed in part to its turning of religious faith into nonnarrative morality, leaving churches with no sense of the sacred and "nothing to offer their members except rallying cries to be good," as Huston Smith puts it.[50]

To reduce the gospel to the "red letters" is to teach the ethics of Jesus, or how to be a moral person, rather than how to be a Jesus person. The whole red-letter movement is a blush on the body. Discipleship is the lifelong process of growing into the person and presence of Jesus. The gospel is not a justice handbook or a superior moral system by which to live. The gospel is your invitation into the story of Jesus and God's actions in history. In the grammar of faith, Jesus is the noun, God is the verb, the Holy Spirit is the adjective, and we are the prepositions (especially "with" and "for").

Until Jesus, we were on opposite sides of the divide between the divine and human. Jesus bridged the human and the divine. Why such trouble speaking well of the bridge that carries us across? Why are so many Christians today temperamentally allergic to the name of Jesus or are passionately airbrushing Jesus out of Christianity? Why is Christology the weak slat under the bed of theology when it should be the whole frame? When Christians start sounding like atheists, arguing that much of what is best about Christianity is unrelated to the life of Christ, it is time to get nervous. Even the chief contemporary rehabilitator of liberalism, theologian Theo Hobson, admits that liberalism went "bad" when it started rejecting its biblical basis and such Christian distinctions as Jesus, God Incarnate, who rose from the dead.[51]

The clearest sign of Christ's ongoing presence in human history is a community of believers, the quality of whose life together shows that divine love can, in fact, transform the world and turn it into God's family.

—Brother John of Taize, *Friends of Christ*

There is a bit of Methodist folk wisdom, falsely attributed to John Wesley, that says the life of faith revolves around three trajectories:

1. Do No Harm

2. Do Good

3. Stay in Love with Jesus (paraphrase of "Attend to all the Ordinances")

It is not enough to live a moral life or to go through life without harming anyone. We are called to do more—to "do good," or as Wesley famously put it (but really didn't) with greater definition, "Do all the good you can. By all the means you can. In all the ways you can. In all the places you can. At all the times you can. To all the people you can. As long as ever you can." Active Christianity is activated by the actions and passions of Christ in the life of a disciple and a Christ-body community.

God made us torches. We've fallen to matchsticks.
God made us geysers. We've fallen to leaks.
God made us His. We've fallen to ours.
God made us humans. We've fallen to humbugs.

—Joe M. Turner

Dressed in his clerical habit, with gown, cassock, and band, the old clerical cap on his head, a Bible in one hand, and a white handkerchief in the other—John Wesley was still preaching from his casket. Wesley's will directed that six poor men should have twenty shillings each for carrying his body to the grave: "I particularly desire that there may be no hearse, no coach, no escutcheon, no pomp except the tears of them that loved me and are following me to Abraham's bosom. I solemnly adjure my executors, in the name of God, punctually to observe this."[52]

The Bible is tied together by stories of people taking what is in their hands, however little or large, and trusting God to make something good of it. In the words of the Sunday school ditty:

> Shamgar had an oxgoad, David had a sling,
> Dorcas had a needle, Rahab had some string,
> Samson had a jawbone, Aaron had a rod,
> Mary had some ointment, and they all were used of God.

That is the biblical understanding of success. If you can take what you have and make do with it for God and good, that's success. If you can't take what you have and make do with it for good and God, that's failure.

Christianity turns the definition of a "viable" social system on its head. It elevates to the upper lofts humility, meekness, mercy, and powerlessness and kicks downstairs hierarchy, wealth, and power. Its primary bonds are not the networks of kith and kin but "brothers and sisters in the Spirit." Its model of governance is a decentralized and transparent body, open and participatory but with a hypercentralized "head" that is Christ. Its loyalty and life is found in the kingdom of heaven, and it lambasts and deconstructs the kingdoms of this world. Its primary success symbol and winning story is of a crucified messiah. We claim the future with the story of a past in which the main character met the death of a common criminal on a cross. Even though we live in a fallen world, where the perversion of the best yields the worst, there is still no excuse for becoming Machiavellian masters of "fallen"[53] power politics rather than masters of the power politics of the Spirit.

All that is sweet, delightful, and amiable in this world, in the serenity of the air, the fineness of seasons, the joy of light, the melody of sounds, the beauty of colors, the fragrance of smells, the splendor of precious stones, is nothing else but Heaven breaking through the veil of this world.

—William Law

The realignment of the soul that comes with Christ living in us is portrayed by Paul as a radical reorganization of the human psyche: "I have been crucified with Christ and I no longer live, but Christ lives in me."[54] When the "I Am" impregnates the id, the soul can forego ego for the supremacy of Christ and his starring role in one's life and personality.

The same radical realignment happens on the We as on the Me level. Paul speaks of the Holy Spirit in Greek as *arrabōn* or "earnest of our inheritance." It is a commercial term that refers to a cash advance or down payment. The life of the church is supposed to be an *arrabōn*, a foretaste of the future, an earnest of eternity, not a complete payment but a guarantee of our inheritance in God's kingdom, a down payment on the divine dream for humanity. But the church doesn't give us it all, or all at once. Augustine never identified the City of God, for example, with the church. In fact, he was careful *not* to identify the two. There is no easy identification of the kingdom of God with the body of Christ. Nothing brings down or messes up the Me/We whole gospel than to confuse God's reign and God's realm, and to allow politics, whether in the church or in the state, to grease the wheels of theology.

Jesus did not come to solve human problems through politics or through wonder-working powers and miracles. The miracles were signs to get people to pay attention and awaken to who he was, to open the door to faith and life and to God's mission in the world. But many couldn't see past the signs to the Signified; many found the signs obstacles rather than openings.

In short, the original Jesus "seminary" for his disciples was basically a course on semiotics. With the Twelve, the Lord of Life conducted a Jesus seminary where Rabbi Jesus gave detailed and personalized instruction on how to read the signs of God's presence and employ signs in reaching others. He immersed his disciples in learning how to decipher the scriptural, the natural, and the cultural signs of God's presence, or to put it more semiotically, he taught us how to climb those "Jacob's ladders" that God drops down from the heavens, how to seek out the stairways that bring us closer to the divine.

It has become SOP (Standard Operating Procedure) to baptize every problem that appears as a "social" problem and summon the state to solve it. The measure of one's compassion and love for justice is measured by the decibels of one's demand for the state to intervene and do something. If the state does not respond, then one's indignation rises accordingly.

Of course, God can use any means God chooses to carry out God's mission in the world. I have made peace with the fact that God must like a lot of people I don't, because God is using people I can't stand, and whose theology is horrid. Or as Richard Baxter put it, God's grace can live with people that I couldn't. In the past, God even used governments to carry out some tasks. God used Cyrus to fulfill a prophecy. God used Assyria and Babylon to carry out a punishment. God used Rome to perform the ultimate sacrificial ceremony. But God used governmental instruments only after God's anointed and appointed instruments were busy with their own missions and not God's mission in the world.

Perhaps the most explosive political issue of Jesus's day: Is it right to pay tribute to Caesar? Here was the landmine to trip all comers. If Jesus said yes, he would alienate his growing following; if he said it was wrong, he would be deemed seditious by the state. We know from Josephus that Galilee was a hotbed of militant activity. Zealots wouldn't even touch a coin with Caesar's superscription on it, much less put a coin in Rome's coffers. Jesus knew the stories of the Galilean freedom fighters and was acutely aware of the political overtones of the Jewish expectations of the Messiah.

Jesus's answer? "Give to Caesar what's Caesars, and to God what's God's."

The bride of Christ was never meant to marry Caesar or any other political entity, although since the fourth century, Christ and Constantine have been having an illicit public affair. The Church is not commissioned to control the state, and the state is not commissioned to control the Church. Jesus rejected the offer of political power from Satan, thus disappointing many who thought he would be a political messiah, and he was put to death for a political crime he did not commit. The church must never allow the hand of Constantine to write any other name but that of Jesus on the throne of the church or onto the heart of Christ's bride.

This book proposes a much-needed broader perspective on three of the most intractable issues of the last fifty years and argues that seeing them as "issues" is precisely part of our problem. A Me/We gospel contends that to live in a different kind of world, we need to see the world in a different kind of way. We need to live in a way that sees Me and We together in a death-till-us-part romance instead of seeing them as opposites that oppose each other. We need to live not as "masters" but as "sojourners and servants" in God's "House and Garden" world. The more we allow our churches and our communities to live a Babel-life, a life of division and separateness instead of a life of wholeness and respect for God's "House and Garden" world, the more we will continue to suffer from the issues that plague us.

Our communities are infected daily by microbes and maladies that break down the health of the body. Terminal illnesses like individualism, racism, consumerism, and environmental degradation bore their way into our being and tear our communities apart. We respond with one-dimensional indignation, theologically shallow activism, stultifying debates, or self-righteous groupthink. We treat marginalized groups as objects for paternalistic intervention rather than as subjects with a role to play in defining their own future, thereby contributing to the oppression and overstructuration of these groups.

By seeing life nonholistically, we have created these black-and-white divisions that prejudice and ail our churches and our communities. And in the plague of consumerism, our self-centeredness takes on scary proportions. How can a Me/We gospel take on issues such as these when all of our attempts have failed? Because a Me/We gospel is not about what we do differently but what we allow God to do instead. Our problem is not that we're not trying hard enough and need to work harder. Our problem is that we not trusting God enough. You reach the heavens not by straining on your tiptoes but by getting down on your knees.

A Me/We Creation Story: Relationships Are Not Black and White

A Birthing Story

Then God said, "Let us make humankind in our image, according to our likeness."

—Genesis 1:26 NRSV

The Illusion of Black and White

Twenty-five hundred years ago, a student of Plato was struggling with the abstract, theoretical, mind-bending concepts of philosophy and mathematics that issued from the mind of this imaginative genius. The student asked Plato, "What practical end do these theorems serve? What is to be gained from them?"

Plato turned to his attending apprentice and rebuked the student, telling a servant, "Give this young man a small coin that he may feel that he has gained something from my teachings."[1]

We needs to challenge Me when you're biting off less than you can chew. But maybe it's time to challenge the master of philosophy himself.

Plato is arguably the most influential philosopher in history. He founded the Academy in Athens, the first institution of higher learning in the Western world. Famous for his allegory of the cave,[2] Plato's most

47

influential allegory, however, may be one most people have absorbed indirectly and don't know it.

Plato once allegorized the human soul as a chariot driven by two winged horses. The horses are from very different pens and must be corralled to work together on the road. The charioteer is the one who gets these opposing forces to cooperate.

In Plato's allegory, one horse is black. The black horse represents our deep but irrational desires and appetites, which threaten to crash the chariot and go out of control. The other horse is white, which represents our better nature—our courage, creativity, and mission. The charioteer is reason personified, whose mission it is to keep both horses in check and pulling together. The white horse you can persuade with argument and reason. The black horse often needs the whip.

Human minds are obscured by familiarity with darkness,
which covers them in a night of sins and bad habits,
and are unable to perceive with the clarity and purity proper to reason.
—Augustine, *On the Morals of the Catholic Church*, echoing Plato

---

Plato's allegory got one thing right. There are two horses. But a gospel embraces, not sublimates or subjugates, the dark horse. A gospel includes the "dark" side of creation in a holistic view of life where the journey toward God is a journey toward the wombs and wells of darkness as well as a quest for illumination and light. We squint into the eyes of the sun. In fact, bright light blinds the eye; half-light blunts the eye; it is darkness that rallies the eye.

Ever watch birds float on the water and then either rise to the sky or dive into the depths? In prayer, we may rise up into the light or go down fearlessly into the dark of the deep. In fact, it is our light sometimes, and not our darkness, that most frightens us. It's easier to keep the lid on our brightness, our talents, our abilities than lift the bushel and "let it shine."

In a gospel, the life of faith is not a simple progression from darkness to light but from the light of truth into the greater light of Truth, from the light of certainty into the darkness of mystery, from the darkness of unknowing into the deeper darkness of the unknown.[3] Conversion may be not just about "seeing the light" as about "seeing in the dark." You can see some things in the dark that you can't see in the light. Faith is only faith when the lights go out. Unless the dark talks to the light, there is no birth.

When were you last snatched into the dark? When were you ever led forward by the lamp of darkness?

The Deep Roots of Racism

Racism will never be erased, but its deepest roots and most sturdily resistant strains, which run through a whole range of human behavior, can be severed when the identification of black with evil and white with good is pulled up and not replanted. There are basically only three positive images of black in circulation: in the black, black card, black belt. Throughout the Christian tradition, there are thousands of examples of black as evil, as in the Augustinian quote above, or the blackness of blind devotion found in Ignatius of Loyola's infamous Rule #13 in the classic "Spiritual Exercises" (1534).[4]

The path we tread is not from darkness to light but from the light of darkness to the darkness of light. A gospel is theologically equinoctial, with day and night of equal length, equal value, and when darkness and light are of equal importance. Without Jesus, day is night, and night is day. With Jesus, day is day, and night is night.

> *I will give you the treasures of darkness,*
> *And hidden riches of secret places,*
> *That you may know that I, the* LORD,
> *Who call you by your name*
> *Am the God of Israel.*
>
> —Isaiah 45:3 NKJV

Nanotechnologists have recently produced a material they call "ideal black" or "Nano-Black." It absorbs 99.9% of light. Christian faith most often is seen as that which reflects Jesus, like the moon reflects the sun. But how can you authentically "reflect" if you have not first "absorbed"? A faith is one that first absorbs as much of the light of Christ as possible until it becomes saturated, and then the "ideal black" soul naturally spills the light of darkness over to others. The star's rays that lead us to Bethlehem never remove the darkness but illuminate the night.

If I ever become a Saint—I will surely be one of "darkness."
I will continually be absent from Heaven—to [light]
the light of those in darkness on this earth.

—Mother Teresa

Mother Teresa came to see the "darkness" as a blessing to her, not because it was of value in and of itself but because she could thus better understand Jesus's misery and suffering while he was on Earth. "I have come to love the darkness—for I believe now that it is a part, a very, very small part of Jesus's darkness and pain on Earth."[5] We are citizens of the light, but we are also denizens of the dark.

Hello darkness, my old friend.

—Paul Simon and Art Garfunkel, "The Sound of Silence"

A whole Me/We gospel, however, requires a nuanced probing of the images of light and dark in scripture, theology, literature, and art. A whole embrace of life includes the dark, not as something always negative but sometimes as positive. In the words of T. S. Eliot's "East Coker":

I said to my soul, be still, and let the dark come upon you
Which shall be the darkness of God.[6]

The Origins of Divisional Thinking

Why do we refine sugar?

One reason, and one reason only. To make it white. So that we can put in our mouths something that is white (and clean), not dark (and dirty). There is no other reason. We like white.

What's wrong with dark sugar? It's dark. We don't like dark. We spend all this extra money, and waste all this extra time, on an unnecessary procedure that makes our sugar white, because we would rather have our sweeteners white, not black.[7]

You know the drill: The universe is locked in a colossal cosmic battle, a war to end all wars. The war has been going on since the dawn of time. It's a war that does not pit nation against nation, or religion against religion. It's a war that pits life versus death, good versus evil, the Lord of Light versus the Prince of Darkness. Lucifer is the "Prince of Darkness," and his minions of evil are the "Dark Force."

There is only one problem: That's Zoroastrianism, not Christianity. Light can be good. But light can be evil as well. The "axis of evil" mentality with its rival forces of light and darkness is one that derives, ultimately, not from Jesus but from Zoroaster.

Sometimes the road leads through dark places
Sometimes the darkness is your friend.

—Bruce Cockburn, "Pacing the Cage"

In Christianity, good and evil are color-rich. Good and evil can both be spiritual or physical. Although some religious groups tend to equate spiritual with good, matter and body with evil, or equate white with good and black with evil, this is manifestly unbiblical. In fact, the association of "night" with "evil" was intensified in the sixteenth century,[8] although it wasn't until the time of the French Revolution that the term *black* for the first time in history began to be used in an ideological sense. The famous witch-hunter's manual *Malleus Maleficarum* (1486) made no big deal of night. But by the time Edmund Spenser was writing his epic poem *The Faerie Queen* (1590)—"Night, thou foule mother of annoyance sad / Sister of heavie Death, and nourse of Woe"—night was evil and diabolical, a place ruled by the Devil where "phantoms of the night" conducted nocturnal acts like pacts with the Devil, the Witches' Sabbath, and sexual revelry.

God's Vision of Unity and Harmony

Hebrew spirituality embraced a holistic view of the divine and the world in which God was sovereign over a unified world, and both dark and light were part of one composite reality. God was the source of both light and darkness. Darkness and light existed in unity and in harmony. All creative acts came from God, all manifestations of One God and one creation, both blessings and storms. This is different from the definitions of devilish evil found in later Christianity or the dualism of Zoroastrianism. The Hebrews simply viewed Yahweh as the source of all created things.

The world was for God's people not a place of dualistic forces but of One force that issues all things across the spectrum of life. Just as in our trinity, we view One God in Three persons, so too did the Hebrews view One God as sovereign over all things good and ill.

We today have so corrupted the definition of *evil* to mean devil-spawned or a separate force working against God that we have trouble imagining the original context. Evil for the early Hebrews essentially meant anything "not good" according to human judgment. God is not merely responsible for the things you approve of but of all things in life. In fact the Eastern mind still sees One God as responsible for all things of the world—good and bad. For the ancient Hebrews good and evil existed in such a reciprocal way that one cannot exist without the other. You cannot have good without its distinguishing bad. You cannot know light without the presence of darkness.

The Hebrew word *ra* does not mean "evil" in that God has created something sinful. God is without sin. Nor does *ra* mean something detrimental or negating of God's nature. God is neither negative nor divisional. God is above all things, and calls all things to himself. "And all things are of God, who hath reconciled us to himself by Jesus Christ, and hath given to us the ministry of reconciliation."[9]

There can be fruit that is good and fruit that is bad (particularly in our judgment). There are acts that appear good to us and those that we don't like. Both come from God in the Hebrew mind-set. The Schema states, "Hear, Israel, the Lord is our God, the Lord is One."

The root metaphor of the word *ra* in Hebrew is "to break." The backstory of the metaphor is the breaking down what stands in the way of God's sovereignty, steadfastness, and goodness. The voice of the Lord breaks the cedars of Lebanon, even as it heals the land. The Lord's voice can break down and build up, can hurt and heal. It can call into being light from the darkness and separate light from dark and yet still call the whole of it "one day."

I form the light and create darkness,
I bring prosperity and create disaster;
I, the Lord, do all these things.

—Isaiah 45:7 NIV

Biblical spirituality is a chiaroscuro spirituality, which knows when to curse the darkness and when to bless the darkness, when to curse the light and when to bless the light. Just as James Joyce framed his writings in a "book of the day" (*Ulysses*) and a "book of the night" (*Finnegan's Wake*), so the psalmist framed life's scourges into terrors of the day that match in horror those terrors of the night: "You shall not be afraid of any terror by night, nor of the arrow that flies by day; of the plague that stalks in the darkness, nor of the sickness that lays waste at noonday."[10]

Jesus Light, Lucifer Light

We think of Jesus as "the Light of the World," but *Lucifer* means "light-bearer" or "shining one" or "morning star" or even "shining star." In Revelation, Jesus himself is identified as the "Bright and Morning Star."[11] So both Jesus and Lucifer are Light-bearers, the "bright and morning stars." But Lucifer is an angel of light for the same reason wolves dress like grandmothers, and demagogues look like statesmen, and Pharisees parade the streets like saints. Manipulation masquerades as adulation, and prejudice disguises itself as justice. Selfishness passes itself off as mindfulness, and wickedness clothes itself in care and concern.

Each "Light-bearer" boasts its own "Light Platform":[12]

1. Lucifer's Light Platform is "You are the Light of the World." Love yourself. Live for yourself. You are number one. You are a god. **The motto of Lucifer Light is "I consume, therefore I am."** Lucifer light is a life focused on self, a life that finds fulfillment in success, consumption, celebrity. But the empire of self is

empty—empty of empathy for others and empty of treasures for oneself.

2. Jesus's Light Mission is "I am the Light of the World." Lose yourself. Give yourself away. Live for Jesus first, then others, then yourself.

   The motto of Christ Light is "I conceive, therefore we are."

   Christ light is a life focused on being, a life that finds fulfillment in beauty, truth, and goodness. Jesus is the light that shines *out of* darkness.

Jesus Darkness, Lucifer Darkness

Can we see Jesus as The Darkness that brings forth Light, as we see Lucifer as The Light that brings forth Darkness?

The Bible is much more complex than light vs. dark. Dark can be evil. But darkness can be good. The dark on your skin is a "beauty mark." But just as dark moles on the face are called "beauty marks," this beauty can turn ugly real fast and be fatal when it becomes cancerous. What Isaiah calls "the treasures of darkness"[13] can quickly become trumperies.

Not Black or White but Blue

It is surprising that no one has done a color-coding of Christianity.[14] If anything, the most "spiritual" color is not white but blue. The "blue hour" occurs just before dawn breaks, when streaks of the color blue appear in the sky as the world brightens again. For those awake to the dawn, it is a magical moment full of the promise and excitement of a new day.[15] The highest state of meditation is known as the "Blue Pearl Meditation," a heightened state of consciousness when your very being appears as a shimmering blue light.[16]

In *Star Wars*, Darth Vader started out with a blue light-saber, but when he went over to the dark side, he had a deep bright red light saber. Sin is crimson. There is not one skin tone in the world described as "crimson," because all humanity shares the red-blooded, red-earthed character of the first man "Adam," whose name in Hebrew means "from the ground" or "red earth." The original source of crimson was the root of a plant used in the indelible marking of animals or property. We have all been "marked" by the original sin of Adam: "In Adam's Fall / We Sinn-ed All." The root of the word *crimson* is the root of the twisted, tangled tree that doomed the human species. But salvation is crimson too. It takes the crimson flow to stem the crimson tide. Out of our blood-red sin, the blood of salvation will redeem God's people. The Lord is our God. The Lord is One.

Awake, O harp and lyre!
I will awake the dawn.

—Psalm 57:8 NRSV

Early to bed, early to rise,
Never get drunk—and advertise.

—"A good motto for a tradesman"[17]

The Crack between Two Worlds

For an example of the complex relationship between light and dark, consider the biblical image of "early and dark," or what the Welsh call "the youth of the day."

Surfers go out early and dark because that's when you get the best waves. Same with hunters. The best time to hunt and fish is early and dark. In fact, the quality of meat depends less on where than when you shoot the animal. Early and dark is when the animal is most relaxed, there is the least adrenaline in the system, and the meat tastes best.

Benjamin Franklin first came up with the idea for putting the clocks forward while in Paris in 1784. Not only were most Parisians not "early birds," but in the words of Simon Reid-Henry,[18] in Paris the "night owls" had "clawed the moral high ground" from the early birds.[19] And yet, most species of birds would never have been discovered if it were not for human "early birds."

There is a "slumber and sleep" lifestyle; and there is an "early and dark" lifestyle.[20] You don't make the most of your life, unless you're willing to discover that time zone the Bible knows as "early and dark."[21]

Most accounts of people's lives before the Renaissance were devoid of personal details.[22] For example, the gospel writers concentrated on Jesus's and his disciples' actions and teachings rather than on the uniqueness of their individual personalities and their personal affairs. Hence it's all the more remarkable that one of the idiosyncrasies of Jesus manifests itself: He liked to get up in the morning when it was "early and dark."

"Early and dark" was the favorite time for Jesus to pray.[23] The resurrection story begins when it was "early and dark."[24] Those who were up and about when it was "early and dark" became the first witnesses to the resurrection. Poet Sylvia Plath says her *Ariel* poems were "written at about four in the morning—that still, blue, almost eternal hour before cockcrow, before the baby's cry, before the glassy music of the milkman, settling his bottles."[25]

Man is an exception, whatever else he is. If he is not the image of God, then he is a disease of the dust. If it is not true that a divine being fell, then we can only say that one of the animals went entirely off its head.

—G. K. Chesterton, *All Things Considered*

Darkness brings the Me and the We together in complex, compelling ways, which is another reason we must learn to see darkness in a positive as well as negative light.

1. Our first journey in life is from darkness to light. Our last journey in life is from light to darkness. We make both of these journeys alone. Every one of us must taste the cup of death. The cup cannot be passed. It must be sipped.

2. Dark energy and dark matter are calling us to come over to the Dark Side. The two most mysterious forces in the universe are "dark energy" and "dark matter." In fact, understanding dark energy and dark matter has been called "the most profound problem in all of science.[26] Understanding darkness may just be the most profound problem in all of theology as well.

What is the universe made of? Atoms, made of electrons and quarks, as well as neutrinos, muons, and gluons, and other charmingly named particles. But if you weighed everything in existence, this is only 4 percent of the total. Ninety-six percent of the universe is composed of things we don't recognize. We don't know what they are. So we call them "dark energy" and "dark matter." More precisely, 22 percent of the universe is made of dark matter, and 66 percent is dark energy. All the matter that "matters" as atoms of "light" is a miniscule part of the universe.[27]

In sum, we live in the dark. What you see is not what you get. To not understand dark energy and dark matter is also to not understand reality. And even science (despite its know-it-allness) doesn't understand reality. Maybe religion and science should talk to one another more than they do, since both have in common that they live to stumble in the dark. In a gospel, faith narratives and fact narratives talk to one another.

Dark energy, also known as antigravity, speeds up the expansion of the universe. Dark matter slows it down and keeps the universe together. They are exact opposites, and we exist because these opposites dance with one another. Forget the "Big Bang." It's really a Big "Ball," a cosmic dance. Once the dance is over, there is nothing. Once the galaxies and galaxy clusters cease their tango of twirls and spins, they will tear themselves apart as they separate.[28] And so we keep dancing in the dark.

Hence I observe how needful it is for me
to enter into the darkness, and to admit the
coincidence of opposites beyond all the grasp
of reason and there to seek truth.

—Nicholas of Cusa (fifteenth century), *The Vision of God*

---

3. Dark is good for us. As we will see, we need the dark to grow. To most of our delight, even dark chocolate is good for us. It is technically a health food, because of its high-density of antioxidants.

We are more familiar with the Isaac Watts song about a land "where infinite day excludes the night, and pleasures banish pain"[29] than we are with the children's song by Elizabeth McEwen Shields, "Do You Know Who Made the Night." But maybe it's time we learned it.

Do you know who made the night? Made the stars and moon so bright? God our Father made the night, Made the stars and moon so bright: Our Father made the night.

Do you know who made the day? Made the glad and happy day? God our Father made the day, Made the glad and happy day: Our Father made the day.

Do you know who made the trees? Waving gently in the breeze? God our Father made the trees, Waving gently in the breeze: Our Father made the trees.[30]

"The Bright Blessed Day, the Dark Sacred Night"[31]

Every Christmas is a war of metaphors. The season of the year that teaches us to wage peacefare rather than warfare is itself a battlefield between "O Holy Night" and "O Holy Nightmare." On one side are the armies of "Holy Light." On the other side are the armies of "Holy Night."

For example, the early Christmas chorale "Christians Awake, salute the happy morn / whereon the Savior of the world was born" volleys against the more familiar "Love came down at Christmas . . . stars and angels gave the sign."

On the side of the "Holy Light" are songs like: "Break Forth, O Living Light of God"; "Break Forth, O Beauteous Heavenly Light"; "O Morning Star, How Fair and Bright"; "I Want to Walk as a Child of the Light"; "Christ Is the World's Light"; "O Come, All Ye Faithful" ("Light from Light Eternal");"O Come, O Come Emmanuel" ("Disperse the gloomy clouds of night, / and death's dark shadows put to flight").

On the side of the "Holy Night" are songs like: "O Holy Night"; "It Came upon the Midnight Clear"; "Watchmen, Tell Us of the Night" ("what its signs of promise are"); "All My Heart This Night Rejoices."

If popularity were the voice of truth, the armies of night would win over light. The most popular Christmas carol of all time? "Silent Night, Holy Night."

Signs of Life: Deep, Dark, Still

A gospel declares a cease-fire in the battle of light vs. dark, white vs. black, day vs. night. *Black* and *darkness* are no more synonyms for everything evil than *white* and *lightness* are synonyms for everything good. Either can be evil or good. When we think of "living water," Jesus's favorite image for his gospel, we think of it as flowing, fast, and clear. Maybe we ought to start thinking of "living water" also as dark, deep, and still. Like Jacob's well, like the Pool of Siloam, underground springs flowing from deep, dark places purified the water.

One does not become Enlightened by imagining figures of light,
but by making the darkness conscious.

—Carl Jung, *Alchemical Studies*

In fact, as the poets have been busy for centuries sounding to dead ears, Jesus did not so much come to flood darkness with light so that darkness is destroyed, as he came to show us how to enter into darkness, and mystery, so that darkness can be explored and experienced.[32] The sun illumines the night; it does not turn night into light.

I want to say to you what I've never said to anyone: why,
in the end, make little children afraid of the dark when one can
soothe them with it and lead them into dreams?

—Sigizmund Krzhizhanovsky, *Seven Stories*

In a gospel, we don't go through life groping in the dark; we grope into the darkness.[33]

At Christmas, it wasn't only light and morn that gave the sign of Jesus's birth, nor was it solely stars and angels that gave the sign of the Savior. It was also beasts that gave the sign; it was also the night that gave the sign. For Jesus was born among the beasts and amid the darkness. As we love to sing, "O little town of Bethlehem, how still we see thee lie; / above thy deep and dreamless sleep the silent stars go by. / Yet in thy dark streets shineth the everlasting light; / the hopes and fears of all the years are met in thee tonight."[34]

Darkness ushered the Messiah into the world, and darkness ushered the Messiah into eternity. Where was God most revealed? Where is God most known? In the darkness of Sinai, of Bethlehem, of Calvary, of the Garden.

It is the darkness in which love is consummated. In birth, in death, and in resurrection, Jesus was swathed in darkness. Jesus was born in a dark cave one night long ago; he died upon a cross where "darkness came over the whole land until the ninth hour."[35] God did the work of resurrection in the hours of night when darkness was deepest: "Early on the Sunday morning, while it was still dark, Mary of Magdala came to the tomb."[36]

Darkness: The Birthing Place

It is good to enter darkness, for darkness is the birthing place where God resides. And where revelations are born. The Hebrew word for *darkness* in Exodus 20:21 (*arafel*) is found in fifteen places in the First Testament, and eight times it refers to the presence of the Holy God.[37] Most people are born at night and are born into eternity at night.

> *Churches are best for Prayer, that have least light:*
> *To see God only, I goe out of sight:*
> *And to scape stormy dayes, I chuse*
> *An Everlasting night.*
>
> —John Donne, "A Hymne to Christ, at the Author's Last Going into Germany"

The gospel of the night is a birthing gospel. When you think of birthing, there is something metaphorically matriarchal about the night—it is mysterious, intuitive, curious, inexplicable. There is something metaphorically patriarchal about the day—it is rational, logical, analytical, clear, well-outlined. Plato described two diverse ways of approaching truth: truth as mythos and truth as logos.

Logos truth is left-brained: scientific, rational, discursive, highlighting reason and science. Mythos truth—*mythos* from the Greek word meaning to close the mouth, shut the mouth, and enter the realms of darkness and speechless wonder—is right-brained: intuitive, silent, hidden, highlighting the emotions and imagination.

> *The Night is mother of the Day,*
> *The Winter of the Spring,*
> *And ever upon old Decay,*
> *The greenest mosses cling.*
>
> —John Greenleaf Whittier, "A Dream of Summer"

The gospel of the night is a developmental gospel. Like the dark room of a photographer's studio, darkness is a light-bringer, a light-birther. Photography is from the Greek meaning "drawing from the light." But the photographic process is really a "drawing from the dark."

Dark rooms are places for creativity, community, and regeneration. Darkrooms develop negatives into positives. In developing film, it takes darkness to develop and make the image clearer. A German diarist in 1944, forced to use candles instead of lightbulbs during nightly air raids, was struck by the difference. "We have noticed," he wrote, "in the 'weaker' light of the candle, objects have a different, a much more marked profile—it gives them a quality of 'reality.'" This quality, he continued, "is lost in electric light: objects (seemingly) appear much more clearly, but in reality it *flattens* them. Electric light imparts too much brightness, and thus things lose body, outline, substance—in short, their essence."[38]

Life needs "dark rooms." Light destroys. It's the darkness that preserves. In the circus, workers talk about having a "dark day." This means a day off . . . and when they go without dark days, they get weary, and circus life becomes almost unbearable.

A medieval monk would labor in dark rooms his entire life transcribing one book of the Bible, never intending his illuminated manuscripts to be seen by anyone other than God and perhaps a priest every now and then. Libraries that own them now keep them in semi-darkness. The only reason you can see the King Tut exhibit is because the artifacts were preserved in darkness. Ditto the Dead Sea Scrolls, which you can only see in the dark when low lights come on for a couple of seconds.

No darkness, no light.

And the people stood at a distance and Moses
approached the heavy darkness where God was.
—Exodus 20:21 AT

Dark caves, like the one in which Jesus was born, or the one in which Jesus was resurrected, are womblike symbols of gestation and germination. Whenever W. H. Auden headed into a dark tunnel by car, the poet always muttered "Hello, mother."[39] We enter life from the dark, and we leave life to enter the dark.

Darkness is the womb in which everything exists. To trust the dark is to trust those deep, underground forces—forces of the earth, the ocean, our genes—that would bring to life the seed that is your soul. God planted deep into the ground of your being the seeds of a one-of-a-kind soul. To grow our soul into the unique creation God intends us to be, we must trust the birthing that is going on inside and around us. We must trust the "fruitive darkness."[40]

Now understand this well: when we turn within ourselves in contemplation, the fruitive unity of God is like to a darkness, a somewhat which is unconditioned and incomprehensible.

—John Ruysbroeck, *The Adornment of the Spiritual Marriage*

Roots lie, and live, in the dark.

I learned a song as a child. But even as a child the metaphor didn't work. It disturbed me:

Kind hearts are the gardens,
Kind thoughts are the roots;
Kind words are the flowers,
Kind deeds are the fruits.

Love is the bright sunshine
That warms into life,
For only in darkness
grow hatred and strife.[41]

No, the darkness is where the roots are found and the nutrients are waiting. Even the Dark Deep Sea is not life barren and species poor but life abundant and species rich. In the deep and in the dark, a vast diversity of life forms have adapted to chemicals as a basis of an entire ecosystem independent of photosynthesis and the sun. All sorts of vents and tubes, polychaete worms and crustaceans, thrive in the dark, whose mysteries we have yet to explore.

Darkness: Time for Dreams

Darkness is down time, and dreaming requires down time, stillness, silence, play. In "a thick and dreadful darkness,"[42] a darkness visible, a darkness risible, God gave Abram a look at the future and his "descendants."

Some cultures are better than others in understanding that the soil of play grows dreams. In Hawaii, the celebration known as the *Alui Po*, or Gathering of Darkness (*Po* means primeval night), is also a gathering of potential and a gathering of dreams. Kumulipo, the teacher of the night, is the source of dreaming, much like the owl of Minerva, the Roman goddess of wisdom and symbol of philosophy, takes flight at night. Christianity has been seduced by philosophical systems that have led it astray because we've refused to get acclimated to the darkness and be instructed by our own "owls of Minerva."

The life of faith requires Night Light. We have made "dark nights of the soul" synonymous with "dry spells of the spirit" when they are in fact growth spurts of the soul and wellsprings of the spirit.

> How weak and little is the light,
> All the universe of sight,
> Love and delight,
> Before the might
> If you love it not, of night.[43]

Light Pollution

Not only can the dark be our primal source of life and creativity, but light can sometimes be our source of pain and death. Perhaps you've heard of light pollution. The brightest light in the sky doesn't come from the Milky Way Galaxy but the nightglow from our biggest cities. It's called "sky glow." Light reflects off moisture and dust in the air, creating sky glow.

In some places of the world you can still see the stars. In Seoul, Korea, at night, all the buildings go dark. In the West Virginia mountains, the darkness is palpable. There is no light pollution in the African dark. On one safari in the African bush, we shut off the engine of our vehicle and sat there in utter silence and darkness for a few minutes, looking at Orion's belt, the A in Taurus, and the Southern Cross.

But for most of the world, sky glow now outshines the moon for nearly half of each month. Chad Moore has taken pictures of darkness at dozens of national parks and has found that it's getting harder and harder to find because the artificial lights from urban centers penetrate even the most remote wild places of our country.[44]

Ninety miles from Las Vegas, the neon lights are lighting up Death Valley National Park. And many of the night creatures are dying because of light pollution. "For species and ecosystems that have evolved with a nightly quota of darkness, light pollution can be a force of ecological disruption."[45]

The biological effects of night pollution on food intake, rates of growth, reproduction, and survival are only now being appreciated. Light pollution is killing the California glossy snake, at one time the most abundant reptile in Southern California. Light pollution is killing the Western long-nosed snake. "Light may interfere with mating activity among diverse nocturnal species, disrupt moth predation by bats, and discourage zooplankton from feeding on algae."[46]

Light can pollute the dark, just like the dark can pollute the light. Too much daylight can intrude on the magic, mystery, and miracle of life. It is the dark that helps us grow. Or as the German artist Peter Weiss puts it: "The bright light blinds / The half-light dulls the edge of things / But darkness challenges the eye."[47]

Why should we wish the darkness harm, it is our element; or curse the darkness because we are doomed to love in it, and die.

—John McGahern, "Along the Edges"

Just as too much physical light can prevent us from seeing in the dark, too many glaring doubts and a mind that looks at everything with a flood-light can prevent us from seeing God and the mysterious presence of the divine in our lives and in our world. God did not create the world as isolated parts but as a unified world that exists in relationship.

In God's world, darkness and light are not opposites nor opposed but in relationship, just as God exists in relationship. In fact, this is our understanding of God too. We see God in the form of a trinity: God the Father, God the Son, and God the Holy Spirit, all various manifestations or understandings of the One and only God.

Darkness and light are relational, as all of creation is relational with itself and with God. In terms of darkness and light, then, it may be helpful to look at the Triune God as (1) the Face of the Deep or Dark (God the Father), (2) the Face of Light (God the Son), and (3) the Face of the Mirror (God the Holy Spirit). God the Creator, the "dark" of origins and womb, is One and in relationship with God the Son, the incarnated Light, brought into being from out of the darkness. It is God the Holy Spirit, the face of the mirror then, which enables us, like the eclipse of the sun, to interact with the Dark and Light at the same time. Of all the mirrors available to humanity, the Face of the Mirror is the only one that tells no lies.

In the beginning when God created the heavens and the earth,
the earth was a formless void, and darkness covered the face of the deep,
while the breath from God *swept over the* face of the waters.
Then God's breath said, "Let there be light," and there was light.
And God saw that the light was good; and God separated the light from the
darkness. God called the light Day, and the darkness he called Night.

—Genesis 1:1-6 NRSV, emphasis added

Face of Darkness

A faith is as much about acclimation to the dark as walking in the blare and glare of light. "Lead, kindly Light," wrote John Henry Newman, "amid the encircling gloom."[48] It's not the dark that's our problem; it's the gloom and despair.

Look out for the words "into the beautiful darkness" in this deeply strengthening and consoling meditation from the best-selling monastic author Macrina Wiederkehr: "Giving yourself up to love is melting into God. It is falling into the hands of the living God with complete abandon. This is the deep, interior prayer for which we have been striving. Here we must let go of our dependency on thoughts, words, and images. We go into the beautiful darkness. We stop struggling. We let the angels carry us. Surrender is the only word we know."[49]

Faith

John of the Cross, arguably Spain's greatest poet, liked to call faith "night to the spirit." Why? Because faith exceeds human understanding, and so it must first darken the intellectual powers before it illumines them. "Faith, manifest, is a dark night for man, but in this way it gives him light. The more darkness it brings upon him, the more light it sheds. For by blinding it illumines him."[50]

He reveals deep and hidden things;
he knows what lies in darkness,
and light dwells with him.

—Daniel 2:22 NIV

Faith is a journey into darkness, because it entails a surrender of ourselves to the unknown, the uncertain, the unmappable, and into the care of God's Spirit. The walk through the night is, as John describes it, a journey of mystery into the sufferings and pain of the world. "For the fruit of the night journey will not be a soiree for a self-preoccupied spiritual elite but the realization that the world's wounds are the spaces through which God graciously enters."[51]

In God's precreation being, God was darkness. The light came out of the darkness.

Absence

Welsh Anglican priest/poet R. S. Thomas writes out of the apophatic tradition, which specializes in "the hiddenness of God, the elusiveness of God, the mystery of God, the silence of God, the darkness of God, even the absence of God." In Thomas's "Via Negativa," he speaks of God as

. . . that great absence
In our lives, the empty silence
Within . . .
. . . .
. . . He keeps the interstices
In our knowledge, the darkness
Between stars.[52]

Hyperpresence

Black is not really a color but actually *all* colors. In that way, it is unique, because it is not itself without all the other colors being present. So it is maybe best described as an über-color but not a color the same way blue or yellow are. Black is all color pigments added together. Mix various paint pigments, and you'll find out quickly enough.

In another sense, black is a heightened presence more than an absence. In 1896, the physicist Gustave le Bon announced to the Academy of Science in Paris the discovery of black light, and the realization that black light is not the absence of light but the presence of minutely small black corpuscles.

Something is clear if it lets light pass through it . . . it doesn't absorb, or reflect. Sometimes we are led forward by a lamp of light. Sometimes by a lamp of darkness.

Mystery

The Bible says "It is [God] who made us, and not we ourselves."[53] But we are afraid of God-made products that are created in the infinite dark where we cannot see or know. We would rather have a "mediated," human-made self than a God-made self. We think we are most ourselves when we are most in control of our lives, not when we are most in God's hands. We prefer a self and a life that we can control, that we can manage and predict, a life that appears as light rather than as dark, a life that isn't built of faith but on sight. We are terrified of God's dark presence in the depths of our being. We are terrified of being fashioned into shapes, of being manipulated into directions we cannot control.

The wisdom of the dark is this: The self is not self-defining. You are not your own. You cannot be anything you want to be. You are created in God's image—whether you want to be or not. God has created you to be a unique you. The fulfillment of your deepest longings and yearnings is not found in fashioning yourself into an image chosen by you but allowing the dark and deep forces of creation to fashion you into God's image for you. If you fail to give birth to what is within you, you die.

Our roots are in the dark; the earth is our country. Why did we look up for blessings—instead of around, and down? What hope we have lies there. Not in the sky full of orbiting spy-eyes and weaponry, but in the earth we have looked down upon. Nor from above, but from below. Not in the light that blinds but in the dark that nourishes, where human beings grow human souls.

—Ursula LeGuin, *Dancing at the Edge of the World*

Awe Inspiring

We are afraid of the dark. So we settle in life for manipulated, manufactured living, for something less than God. We attempt to make ourselves, or we turn over our freedom to others, to society, to spouses, to significant others, to social forces, and allow them to carve us into a convenient shape and then drop us noiselessly into some niche where we are to stay lodged for the rest of our lives. Just as darkness and chaos go together, light and law go together in the First Testament (e.g., Ps 19). Darkness is the chaos that precedes creation and light. It was out of the darkness, we are told, that God formed light; it was out of chaos that God created the cosmos.

To affirm the darkness is to submit one's life to forces and powers higher and deeper than one's own—to trust the unmediated, uncontrollable, unpredictable presence of God. We must come to welcome darkness if we are to welcome the dark birthing processes of life.

Black is the color of blind faith.

—Lori Wagner

The darkness of the monastery matches the monastic vow of silence and the monk's openness to unknowing. Monks teach us that sometimes it is better to say nothing, because there is too much to say.

The poet Rainer Maria Rilke, whom Robert Bly calls the most important poet of the last five hundred years, tells us that the origin of this birthing darkness is God:

> my God is dark, and like a webbing made
> of a hundred roots, that drink in silence.[54]

Or again:

> You darkness, that I come from,
> . . . .
> I have faith in nights.[55]

Gift of Darkness

A whole gospel thanks God for the gift of night, the gift of darkness. It doesn't try to control it or force it into light. It is the gift of night—its sleep and subconsciousness, its physical rejuvenation and spiritual refreshment—that re-creates us for a new day, and that gives meaning to our days. It is that gift of night, the silence of dreams, visions, angelic visits, revelatory events; that is, making you into you and not into someone else, literally. W. H. Auden wrote a thank-you poem to Sigmund Freud for opening up the dreaming of the night and its role in the formation of the id sense of identity:

> but he would have us remember most of all
> to be enthusiastic over the night
> not only for the sense of wonder
> it alone has to offer, but also
>
> because it needs our love.[56]

Formative Darkness

From out of our "birthing spaces" in which we spend intimate space with God, our prayer spaces, our "Shekinah" moments, our identity as God's people is birthed and formed. God forms within us a Me identity and a We identity, a uniqueness and a sense of belonging to something much bigger than ourselves.

A mother was determined to instill a sense of confidence in her children at the earliest possible age. As soon as her first child was old enough to respond, she began to ask him, over and over again, "Why do I love you?"

She taught him to answer: "Because I'm Matthew."

When the mother's second child, Lillian, was old enough, she tried the same dialogue. "Why do I love you?" she asked.

Without hesitation Lillian responded, "Because I'm Matthew."

Why does God love all us Matthews, all us Marys, all us Toms, all us Marthas? Because you're you. Because I'm me. Because you're the Mary God needs. Because I'm the Len God needs.

Once we have come to terms with the divine ownership and sanctity of We and Me, we need to take We and Me one step further. Who is included in this We and Me? Notice until now how we have defined We—only in human terms. This is not biblical.

Oh Lord, how manifold are your works!
In wisdom you have made them all;
the earth is full of your creatures.

—Psalm 104:24 NRSV

God created a world of livingness of which humanity is a part. Each covenant is made with all of creation. God's universe is a unity of many as one, an entire created world of individuality in relationship, each thing formed, created, breathed, claimed by God. We are part of a glorious interwoven tapestry designed by our Creator. Each of us is a colorful and unique strand in a multitude of colors, patterns, movements, weaves. And We are being forever formed, one by one, by the mysterious, creative, midwifing hand of our Maker.

Comedian Dick Van Dyke tells the story of a little boy who figured out how babies get their belly-buttons. "You see," he announced, "When God finishes making little babies, God lines them all up in a row. Then God walks along in front of them, pokes each one in the tummy with His finger, and say, "you're done, . . . and you're done, . . . and you're done."[57]

The darkness of formation is good, for it reminds us that God is constantly poking a finger into the soil of our soul and the soil of creation, and saying, "you're not done . . . and you're not done . . . and you're not done."

You may think you know all there is to know about you, about me, about creation. But the true knowledge of God is this: You don't know; you're not done. God's ways are inexhaustible, unimaginable, unknowable, incomprehensible. Indeed, if God were simple enough for us to understand, God would be too simple to have created you or me or this universe. Albert Einstein used to joke that the most incomprehensible thing about the universe is that it is at all comprehensible.

It is when things go wrong, when the good things do not happen,
when our prayers seem to have been lost, that God is most present.
We do not need the sheltering winds when things go smoothly.
We are closest to God in the darkness, stumbling along blindly.

—Madeline L'Engle, *Two-Part Invention*

70

Tenebrae is Latin for "darkness." In the Tenebrae service, which takes place in Western Christianity during the late evening or early morning of the last three days of Holy Week (Maundy Thursday, Good Friday, Holy Saturday), all the candles are slowly extinguished except for the highest candle. Here is Jesuit priest George Tyrrell's (1861–1909) recollection of this evening office and its mirroring of the lengthening shadows of life:

> As at Tenebrae, one after another the lights are extinguished, till one alone—
> and that the highest of all—is left, so it is often with the soul and her
> guiding stars. In our early days there are many—parents, teachers, friends,
> books, authorities—but, as life goes on, one by one they fail and leave us
> in deepening darkness, with an increasing sense of the mystery and inex-
> plicability of all things, till at last none but the figure of Christ stands out
> luminous against the prevailing night.[58]

Face of Light

What I tell you in the dark, speak in the daylight;
what is whispered in your ear, proclaim from the roofs.

—Matthew 10:27 NIV

After the black of transcendence comes the white of immanence.

White is the presence of all the colors of light. Only full-spectrum light is healthy. Plants can be killed by "malillumination," a word coined by John Ott in 1956 to describe the bad effects of standard lights, which are heavy on yellow with almost no blue.

A Me/We gospel involves a life of heliotropic holiness. The word *helio-tropic* comes from "helio" for sun and "tropic" for turn. Heliotropic is usually used in the context of gardening, as plants are aggressive sun seekers. But the word is even more appropriate in the context of faith formation, for the soul is an aggressive Son seeker. In the words of organic theologian Robert Dale, "To constantly face our source of power and inspiration is a key to growth and change. Like sunflowers, leaders are sun-chasers. We recognize clearly where our light comes from."[59]

We weren't meant to stay in the dark. There is a reaction against indus-trialized farming for a reason. On industrial farms, chickens are raised exclu-sively in the dark. Because when it's dark, they don't move; and if they don't move, they grow fatter faster. In just six weeks they can go from a little chick to a three-to-four-pound chicken. No light, no movement. We stay in the dark, and we grow fat in our sinfulness and selfishness.

But while the plant's limbs reach for the light, the whole plant isn't in the light. The roots of heliotropic holiness are in the dark. Roots grow in the dark. Birth takes place in the cave, in the darkness of the womb.

The darker the night, the brighter the stars. The deeper the roots, the higher the promise of bloom and beauty. One Christmas not too long ago a woman was trying to break multiple addictive cycles and was seeking God in the midst of pain and struggle. She called me all excited. . . . She had an epiphany during Epiphany. And her epiphany was this: In order for the wise men to see the stars that led them to Jesus—it had to be dark. Darkness helps us see the stars that ultimately lead to Jesus. The light is found only in the darkness, just as peace is found only through suffering.

The light is at the heart of the dark; the dawn breaks when
we have entered fully into the night.

—Rowan Williams, *Open to Judgement*

Children of the Light and Dark

The Transfiguration was less something that happened to Jesus than to the disciples, whose eyes were opened and transformed so that they could see what Christ had always been—a shining beacon, full of light. They were able to see what was always there, but they had been unable to see until the dark-ness led them into the light.

We live as "children of light . . . for the fruit of the light is found in all that is good and right and true."[60]

"Whoever loves a brother or sister lives in the light."[61]

We are "children of light" (*lucis filios*), the light that shines in the dark-ness, serving a God who says "I am light" in whom "there is no darkness at all."[62] Or in the words of the psalmist: "The darkness is no darkness with thee; the night is as clear as the day."[63] To be a child of the light is to be re-created, every creation an act of re-creation, or God-creation from out of the darkness.

Once you were darkness, but now in the Lord you are light.
Live as children of light—for the fruit of the light is found
in all that is good and right and true.

—Ephesians 5:8-9 NRSV

But we are also "children of dark," or as Paul put it, people who see through a glass darkly. Followers of Jesus are people who let darkness shine on the mystery. It is a mistake to think only the mystics valued darkness, although they could be most vocal about it.[64] Witness the anthems to the night[65] by two sixteenth-century saints—Teresa of Avila (1515–1583) and John of the Cross (1542–1591). In his poem "Dark Night," John praised the dark in language eerily anticipating the second act of Richard Wagner's *Tristan und Isolde* (1865): "Oh, night that guided me, Oh, night more lovely than the dawn, Oh, night that joined Beloved with lover, Lover transformed in the Beloved!" But John Donne's "Hymn to Christ" (1619) asserts that "Churches are best for Prayer, that have least light; / To see God only, I go out of sight: / And to escape stormy days, I choose / An everlasting night."[66] Roman Catholic theologian Karl Rahner called God "ineffable darkness." "All I know is a door into the dark," confesses the Nobel Prize–winning Irish poet Seamus Heaney.[67] And that door leads us into the presence of a God who is first found in the dark.

When creation began, "darkness covered the face of the deep."[68] In creation, God did not bring the chaos into order so much as God allowed the chaos to play in the light rather than bang around in the dark.

English playwright and screenwriter Peter Barnes's monologue "The Slaughterman" tells the story of the deconversion of a slaughterman from slaughterhouse economics and slaughterhouse theology. In his pre-deconversion days, when "I slaughtered by day and studied the Torah by night," the Slaughterman relates how "In the Torah nothing is accidental. God, whose words are the instrument of *His* work, created the world through words. God said, 'Let there be light,' and there was light. If He had said another word then the result would've been different. He could've said 'Let there be soap,' or 'Let there be kraplash.' Then where would we've been?"[69]

Light was the first creation. When God wanted company in the universe, God created light. The unknown became known. "Word" became flesh. Or story became storyteller. Everything began in darkness. When there was nothing but God, there was only darkness (Gen 1). On the first day God created light. God separated light from the primeval darkness, and "God called the light Day, and the darkness he called Night" (Gen 1:5 NRSV). The dark gave birth to the light.

In the Christian tradition, revelation is understood as an experience of light. Light is God's self-communication. When God separates the light from the dark, that's revelation. Revelation takes place in the space between. To live in Christ is to live in the light. But revelation, or the "separating briefly" of darkness from light through allowing for space between them, is still unity. It is revealing something to us who see in part. We cannot see well the "wholeness" that is God, so that in the garden, when we eat of the Tree of Life, wholeness is separated, and we "see" things as separate rather than whole. This relational unity is the essence of covenant and the beauty of revelation: A slight separation allows us to "see" and experience God but only in relationship with God. Covenant (in Hebrew terms) is two in unity with space between them.

Using the biblical metaphors precisely then, God is the night that lights the night.

Jesus: The Light of the World

Just as precisely, Jesus is the light that nights the light. Jesus is the refraction of the divine Person that allows us to see and experience God.

God in three persons is God whether we see God through Jesus or experience God through the power of the Holy Spirit. Jesus is God revealed, as light reveals what is in the dark.

Put philosophically, darkness is nothing more than the absence of light—darkness is not "caused" except by the removal of light. Cold is not an entity; it's the absence of heat. Dark is not an entity; it's the absence of light. Fear is not an entity; it is the absence of love.

Put scientifically, light only reveals things that are already there in the darkness. Light does not bring anything new—it only reveals things not seen before, and threads together space and time. Through light things are shown in their relation to one another. In the words of Lawrence Krauss, "the trajectories of light rays give us a map of space-time just as surely as warp and weft threads elucidate the paths of a tapestry."[70]

Jesus is the sun, and the scriptures are the moon. The gospel (Wisdom) of the light is this: *You are not alone.* The dark or mystery of existence is revealed through relationship with the light.

Jesus is the true light coming into the world and giving light to all.[71] Jesus has never left the world. The light is still coming, the incarnation is ongoing, and giving light to everybody. Jesus, the Light of God, shows what is there all the time: A God who created us and who loves us with a passion. Through the light of Christ, God revealed the truth that we are meant for God. The "light of God's face" was Jesus Christ. Our only happiness, our true joy, is when God's light shines on us and we lift up "the light of [God's] countenance" on others.[72] The incarnational is that which already exists in the dark brought into the Light. That's how Jesus is part of the origin-al God.

When we come "out of darkness into [God's] marvelous light,"[73] we see two things we could never see before. These two things constitute the double meaning of the word "light:" (1) truth and (2) levity. Our night-God becomes known to us in the works and wonders of light-Christ, the Sun of Righteousness, and in the incarnations of the divine in human life through the nightlight of the Holy Spirit and the "nocturnal writings" (as one biblical scholar calls them) of the gospels.

Is it any wonder the Light causes saints to levitate and clowns to leap?

The Big Ball

Light is the creative principle behind and in all things. The Big "Ball" describes the creation of the universe from the light of two atoms coming together to dance. But the Big Ball does not just happen once. The Big Ball happens at every birth, as two single cells, one cell from the father, one cell from the mother, come together in an explosion of dancing gametes that gushes forth a galaxy of nuclear, cytoplasmic, and membranous material.

Now can our eyes spring free to see the night.

The sun is strong, I'm standing in the light
I wish to God that it were night.

—Bob Dylan, "Nettie Moore"

Light promotes organic growth. The sun, our source of light, is the greatest energy source in the Milky Way Galaxy. Light makes us joyful and generative. Light comes as both wave and particle, and it travels faster than anything in the known universe. Concentrated light creates fire, and sets us on fire. In this way the believer does not simply have joy. The believer is joy. The Christian is to be joy, not merely have joy. The "Father of lights" has given us the revealing light of Christ. And the light of Christ should set us on fire. Even as we bask in the light of Jesus, we become part of the light.

Do not metals and precious stones begin to shine when we polish them?
Are not clear windowpanes manufactured from sand and ashes?
Is not fire struck from black coal? And is not this luminous quality
of things evidence of the existence of light in them?

—St. Bonaventure

In thy light do we see light?[74] We love to think about basking in the light. But if anything, we ought to fear the light more than the dark, for it is the light that carries judgment with it.[75] Once we've seen the light, we are thereafter judged severely when we fail to recognize the Light. We also have the responsibility to act according to the light imparted to us.[76] We forget too readily that the "Day of the Lord" is a day of judgment.

We fear the dark for another reason: we are afraid to use anything but our eyes to see in the dark. Persons who are blind have a facility known as "facial vision," but it's an incredible gift all of us have been given. It is what happens when a sighted person tries to walk through a dark room at night. Concentrate on the darkness with ferocity of focus, and you eventually can feel the objects in front of you without having to see them. The real enemy is not darkness but fear of the dark.

One place where we are most vulnerable to judgment is the way in which the human species can be quite specious. Humans are not the only characters in God's redemption story. In the garden of Eden, Adam and Eve speak the language of the beasts, and live in harmony with creation. Psalm 36:6 praises a God who "saves humans and animals alike" (NRSV).

The only eagle some people want to save and protect is the one on the back of a dollar bill. Noah honored a God who made a covenant promise with all of creation, and then kept it. Noah is a savior figure not just for humans, or for animals, but for every living thing. Noah saved the ecosystem, of which we humans are a part. For we are nature; we are nature come to consciousness. We are the cambium of nature. We have no problem hearing the sound of these words—"sovereignty of nations." But when we put together these words, the charge of pantheism or pan-entheism is levied: "sovereignty of nature." Humans and humus, the earth from whence we came, share a common destiny. You can't have a sick earth, a sick climate, a sick planet, and a well people.

Signs of God's Redemption Story

The biblical kingdom of God is "a new heaven and a new earth." The gospel of the light announces that the whole earth is part and parcel of the redemption story. That is one reason why the bread of our communion with Christ is shaped in a circle: to symbolize the redemption of the entire cosmos. The whole creation awaits its transformation, transfiguration, and transubstantiation with eager longing and expectation.

One sees this hope in both the First and Second Testaments, where redemption returns balance and harmony and beauty to creation: "the wolf lives with the lamb, / the panther lies down with the kid;"[77] "the universe, all in heaven and on earth, might be brought into unity with Christ."[78] We have sung this hope in our hymns, both ancient and new: "All Gloria in excelsis cry, Heaven, earth, sea, man, bird, and beast, He that is crowned above the sky. *Pro nobis Puer natus est.*"[79]

The hymn "Now All the Woods Are Sleeping," originally written by Paul Gerhardt in 1648, and adapted musically by J. S. Bach in 1729, begins with "sleeping woods" in the "night and stillness" and ends with "happy slumbers":

The last faint beam is going,
The golden stars are glowing
In yonder dark-blue deep;
And such the glory given
When called of God to heaven,
On earth no more we pine and weep.[80]

Face of the Mirror

Humans are made in the image of God. That doesn't mean God looks like us. But it does mean that our thoughts and emotions have their source in God's thoughts and emotions, and that we reflect back to God the creativity out of which we were created.

Genesis 1 begins in a mirror image, the water, as God's Spirit dances over the surface of the mirror and separates like from darkness. We are created imago Dei, in the holism of dark and light, and we manifest both the light and dark of the divine. Jonathan Edwards conceived a theological notion he called "remanations." A *remanation* is the human response to a divine "emanation," the mirroring of the divine presence in our midst.

According to Edwards, when a human encounters the emanation of the divine, the human spirit responds with its own reflection, its own kind of bounce-back echo, of that divinity. Of course, the emanation Edwards meant was the person and presence of Jesus Christ. Each human being who encounters the Christ, who is transformed in the presence of that divine emanation, becomes a "remanation"—a reflection of that glory. The Holy Spirit is the ground sand, polished metal, or precious silver that binds as it reflects, allowing us to see that the "Father and I are One."

Madame Day holds classes every morning,
Professor Night lectures each evening.

—Psalm 19:1-2 *"The Message"*

Let There Be Links

The second-to-last plague that hit ancient Egypt has always mystified me. Because of Pharaoh's pride and Moses's faithfulness, the ancients were inflicted with ten terrifying plagues. Even today, with our slasher movies and

Armageddon plots, these plagues send chills up the spine. Water turned to blood. Swarms of frogs, gnats, flies, and locusts covered everything. Blistering boils. Dying cattle. And of course the final tragedy, the death of all first born—unless protected by a blood-painted doorframe to signal the angel of the Lord to "pass over" the household.

But there is one plague that stands out as strange, almost benign, to our twenty-first-century sensibilities: The plague of "darkness." What's so bad about darkness?

For those of us who grew up or still live in lands far from the equator, "darkness" is a big part of each year. Days of "night" dominate life for three to five months, depending on your latitude. So what's a little darkness?

What's a little darkness? The worst plague of all, if you were the equatorial Egyptians. For them light was a God—"Amun-Ra," to be exact. According to Egyptian theology every night the sun, "Amun-Ra," died. That word "died" was more than a metaphor. Every night Amun-Ra died. Every morning Amun-Ra was reborn.

No daily resurrection of Amun-Ra, no life. Amun-Ra was the source of light, heat, food, everything. Amun-Ra brought the crops to harvest and dictated the annual floods of the Nile that restored the soil. Amun-Ra brought to Egyptian culture its order, stability, and rhythm, a culture that flourished almost unchanged for over 10,000 years.

There was only one alternative to the daily order of Amun-Ra: Chaos. Chaos was a nonworld, a noncreation, a place unknown, unpredictable, dark, and without form. The forces of this Chaos lurked forever on the fringes of Egyptian culture, threatening to overwhelm and overtake order. Chaos was kept at bay only by the power and perfect predictability of Amun-Ra.

There were . . .

No light switches to flick on.

No street lights to show the way.

No oil lamps to carry with you.

So imagine yourself living in Egypt when Moses called down the plague of darkness. But for the Egyptians, this was more than an inconvenience or agricultural snafu. It was the ultimate victory of a God they did not know or understand. The mysterious, chaotic, uncontrollable, and powerful darkness of Yahweh overcame the Egyptian sun god during that plague.

The "darkness" of God the Creator began "re-creating" their predictable world into something unfamiliar, and the Egyptians were soon blanketed within the power of this Hebrew God who had enveloped their reality with darkness.

Only darkness, and deep darkness at that, even at mid-day. Even all day. No day. No night. Only dark.

The blackness did not just bring with it a child's fear of things that go bump in the night. That impenetrable dark meant the end of the world. Amun-Ra had died and was not being reborn. The powers of chaos had won. No longer was there a world, a creation. As the Egyptians knew and understood it, the plague of darkness signaled the end of all existence—both the here and the hereafter.

Could anything be more terrifying? Could any story be more life-destroying, more hope-extinguishing, than this one? The plague of darkness was not just something the Egyptians had to "live through." The plague of darkness took away any reason to live, any reason for being. The plague of darkness was a plague directed not at the body but at the soul.

While dreaming, perhaps, the hand
of the sower of stars caused the forgotten music to sound.

—Antonio Machado, as translated by Peter Klausmeyer

Sticky Resonance

But we are a people who embrace both darkness and light, both night and day. In God's first moments, as God's voice sang creation into existence, God created darkness and light to exist together in harmony, forever in relationship with each other. In a sense, our soul was meant to resonate with the sounds of existence—the sounds that make up a world that sings with a symphony of differences. We are a plethora of Me voices praising God in a reverberating We chorus—all echoing in tone and image with the Creator's voice.

God's voice is what holds all the pieces of the universe together in a "sticky resonance." Night and day, black and white, deep and wide, water and sky, creature and human, root and flower. We are a magnificent symphony of creative energy. To divide and polarize light from dark is to destroy the beauty of its symmetry and the richness of its resonance. All creation is a series of linked relationships. Just as God is One, creation is a great unity of all individually created parts, held together by relational bonds that connect more through what you can't see than what you can.

Love connects you in a harmonious and eternal concatenation of links that bring you together in joyous and everlasting communion.

—John Smallman

Today we know a lot about light. We know the speed at which it travels (186,000 miles/second, or 671 million miles/hour). We know it comes on when we pull a plug or throw a switch. We know it describes potato chips that taste really bad. But the most important thing we know about light is what makes light "light:" links. Light only comes about through links, through relationships. Interlinked frequencies communicate and emit different kinds of light—ultraviolet, infrared, a rainbow spectrum of colorful relationships. Light is formed by the connection between frequencies, the relationship between particles. The links give us the light that transforms our world. Maybe a better translation of "Let there be Light" is "Let there be Links."

We see God as Light because the links are what connect us to the triune linkage. In the Christian tradition, revelation is understood as an experience of light even though most revelations from God come "in the dark." The difference between "God is nowhere" and "God is now here" is but the addition of a link, a space of light, a span of relationships. Creation itself was the first self-revelation of God. When God separates light from dark, refracts it to make it easier for us to see, what we remanate to the world is the light incarnated from the darkness, so that we can be linked to God. Refraction is revelation.

81

Unity of Linkage

You and I are the links. Just as in creation, light separated from dark allows us to see the different Mes within the We; we also need to see the unity of their linkage. Refraction doesn't separate light from dark but bends it to allow us to see both better. Christians especially should not be afraid of the dark, for out of the dark comes the Light of Christ. From our blind faith comes the startling, shining colors of the reflecting kingdom. A gospel discerns the links within the darkness through faith.

What makes darkness so terrifying is that we can no longer see things in their relationship. Everything appears de-linked. Has there ever been a child who has never been afraid of the dark? We've always told our kids this double-edged "good news:" "there is nothing that exists in this world that isn't present both in the dark and in the daylight." For kids, that is supposed to mean there are no magical creatures that only appear to terrorize children at night. For parents, that message serves to remind us, we must always be on our guard. Parents know that God is as present in the darkness as in the light.

To me, every hour of the light and dark is a miracle,
Every cubic inch of space is a miracle,

—Walt Whitman, "Miracles"

There is no inborn, universal fear of the dark. A fear of this blanket of blackness is linked to our fear of linking with the unknown.

Many say John 3:16 is the most perfect encapsulation of the good news of the gospel: "For God so loved the world that he gave his only Son, so that everyone who believes in him may not perish but may have eternal life" (NRSV).

It is good news. It is the best news. But it is not the only news. The news is not just that God loves the world. The news is not just that because of this love God gave his Son. This news also reports that "everyone who believes in him" may enter and enjoy a new kind of linkage, a link called "eternal life."

Yes, But . . .

But wait a minute: The good news has a qualification.

To demonstrate what this new, extraordinary relationship entails, John's

Gospel immediately goes back to the competing images of darkness and light. Those "in darkness" are not "in him." Those who live in the light are "in God." Light is created out of relationships. Light is about links. A life lived according to the light, "in the light," a life lived "in Christ," is a life lived in conscious relationship with God. But we fear what we don't know (in the dark). We fear living "by faith and not by sight." We fear living without signs of God's presence, and light provides the links that God uses to reveal God's presence. The Light of Christ is the link that connects us to a God who is dark to us. His light is our flashlight, and when we come into the Light, we see God better. That's why to live in the Light is to live in Christ, the incarnated revelation of the darkness of Three in One. Those who remain in darkness are those who don't know Jesus.

Goethe, the German philosopher, once cried out "Light, Light, more Light." Unamuno, the Spanish thinker, commenting on Goethe's plea, protested: "No, it is warmth, warmth, and more warmth. We die of the cold, not the darkness. It is not the night that kills us but the frost." A life lived in the dark is dangerous, not because the dark is bad or evil but because we can forget in the dark the warm links of the light. We do "evil," or morally ambiguous things, "at night," because in the darkness, we feel we can de-link, we can become disconnected to the rest of the relationships in our lives. Living in the "mystery" and being good "stewards of the mystery" is not living in hiding but living in faith. This is the meaning of *alētheia*, the Greek word for "truth:" to come out of hiding. The Bible is a hide-and-seek story where God is the Seeker, and we are the hiders.

Nobody understands this moral truth quite so well as Las Vegas, which has come up with a perfect twenty-first-century rendition of John 3:19-21: "What happens in Vegas, stays in Vegas." In the city that is known for going and flowing in the dark, "What happens in Vegas, stays in Vegas" is a slogan that pretends that what happens "in the dark" does not impact our "real" life, our "relational" life, our "link" life.

But like we tell our kids . . . everything that exists in the daylight *is* there in the dark, and everything that happens in the dark is still present in the daylight. We cannot escape our knowledge of good and evil and de-link from God or from each other. We cannot pretend to be one thing in the daylight and another in the darkness.

Authenticity is the ascending spiral of coming out of hiding, out of the darkness of origins and into the Light of new beginnings, and then the dance from darkness to light starts again. You don't so much replace dark with light as bring the darkness into light. Faith is connective; unfaith is delinking ("Adam, where are you?"). While we need to be born and dwell in God's darkness, we need to be redeemed and walk in God's Light.

The greatest delusion of both the light and the dark is this: that you can de-link from everyone else, that you are the center of the universe, which now becomes your "youniverse." In this Luciferian universe, you think that you are all that matters, that everything that exists is there to meet your needs. Without the Me/We of light and dark, without points of reference outside yourself, you start to think that nothing matters beyond your desires.

Galileo was wrong.
I am the center of the universe.

—T-shirt

There can be a Me dark and a We relational dark, a Me light and a relational We light. When only what you want matters, whether in the blinding dark or the blinding light, there is total disregard for every other person and the planet. It is not enough to say that this Las Vegas "youniverse" has mistaken the search for personal fulfillment with the search for God. It is more accurate to say that in this de-linked, selfie world, we have come to think of ourselves as gods, who are entitled to whatever we want, everyone and everything else be damned. There is nothing more repulsive than a human being totally self-absorbed.

No wonder this Youniverse is filled with narcissists who see themselves as the navel of the universe.

No wonder this Youniverse is filled with solipsists who are totally in love with self, selfies who can't see anybody else but themselves.

No wonder this Youniverse is filled with goddifiers, who believe in themselves, not in the God of heaven and earth; goddifiers believe only in the god of themselves, where everything is permitted, nothing is taboo, and anything goes in the pursuit of calling out your name in the dark.

No wonder this Youniverse is filled with islanders, who choose to do the two worst things you can do in life: refuse to link and refuse to be linked.

No wonder this Youniverse is filled with "Las Vegans," who do what is right in their own eyes.

Oh, by the way, this singularity Youniverse is the biblical definition of hell.

God's love of this world requires us to come into the light (John 3:16). But that requires a Copernican Revolution, one that would remove the Me from the center of the universe and reposition in its place a "world, in which everything doesn't orbit around a single person's wishes.

We Have a Choice

Let there be Light. Let there be links.

Or . . .

Let there be the "lights" of "Las Vegas." Let there be a de-linked Youniverse.

"When does night become day?" an old proverb asks.

The answer? "When you can look into a person's eyes and see a brother or sister."

The answer? When you can see the links.

A gospel is a whole gospel for a whole world. Relationality is not black or white but a rainbow of relationships and an economy of links. We are part of God's created world, and the more we link together, the more diverse and creative we can be.

As we grow together in a God-infused identity, we begin more and more to resemble a "whole" people, not divided, not dualistic, but a people, both black and white, who embrace the relationality of God and all that is in God's image. We need as God's people to move our communities from the divisions of deep racism to the joy and blessings of a deep and connective faith.

A Me/We Economy: Christians Don't Consume, We Conceive

A Garden Story

The Lord God took the man and put him in the garden of Eden to till it and keep it.

—Genesis 2:15 NRSV

"As a Person Conceiveth (or Consumeth) in His Heart, So Is He"

We cannot do what we want with creation any more than we can do whatever we wish with our own souls. Creation is not our own, just as our souls are not our own. They both belong to God, because God created us, redeemed us, and re-dreamed us. In the words of the Deuteronomic code: "When you are trying to capture a city, do not cut down its fruit trees, even though the siege lasts a long time. Eat the fruit, but do not destroy the trees; the trees are not your enemies."[1]

Destroying the trees is like taking your own life. Shooting yourself in the foot, as you would have it. "Do not damage the fruit, the trees, the roots, the soil that nourishes you and of which you are a part" in fact is a metaphorical way to say "keep God's covenant, your life depends upon it." Keep your

87

relationship with God rich, nourished, blooming, fruit-bearing, no matter what else happens in the course of your days. "Tend" it well.

But the scriptures don't stop there. It's not enough just to keep things "tight" with God. No garden grows merely by protecting the seeds and plants and tending their roots. We are also called to "till" the soil. To cultivate it, dig into it, turn it over, expand the fields, pass on the knowledge of how to tend the crops, so that fruit bearing will go on throughout many generations.

In the language of siege, not only do you not destroy the trees but also you plant new ones, and cultivate the spreading of the ones that are there. You don't just keep things static; you encourage growth, expansion, even greater health. You make things flourish. You keep the cycle of rebirth going. In the case of the covenant, you plant the seeds of God's love and presence into the hearts of others, so that not only you but also many will bear fruit going forward. We are called to keep, remember, cherish, remind ourselves of the story, and we are called to cultivate the story in others. We are called to pass on the story, the relationship, the sacredness, the joy of garden living, so that everyone can be part of God's "House and Garden."

A Garden World and a Me/We Economy

A "House and Garden" life is about caring for our relationship with God, out of which all Me/We relationships spring forth. Words can't penetrate to the mystery of our being. Only stories and metaphors can bring an apprehension and appreciation of life. That's why our early scriptures were written in a rich vein of story and metaphor. In our Genesis story, the agricultural metaphor of the garden is the preeminent metaphor, becoming a presiding metaphor of the story. In Hebrew faith, we are called through the metaphor of the garden to "till" and "keep" our covenant relationship with God. And we are called to let that relationship be a part of all of the others we engage in.

In the garden story, we experience our broken relationships: our relationship with God, our relationship with ourselves, our relationship with each other, and our relationship with the whole of creation. Expelled from the garden, humans spent centuries trying to go it alone, plowing with broken wheels, until Jesus made it easy for us once again to share that yoke and steer that plow. Jesus lifts the burden of our brokenness and gives us a way to reconnect with God and each other in health and harmony.

As for "tilling and keeping" God in our lives, Jesus can now help do it for us and with us. If we are living a garden life, then Jesus is our living water, the soil of our soul, our superfood (Bread of Life), and our rototiller to weed out the weeds and plant the seeds deep. Problem is, some of us are still stubbornly trying to either plow our own fields with hand and fist, or we are forgetting the fields altogether, seeking to "buy" or "make" our own food in the ways of the super-duper Market.

Weeds are flowers too, once you get to know them.

—A. A. Milne

In the departure from the covenant that binds Me to God and We to one another and the earth, a broken set of relationships are born. Out of these come some of the most insidious dysfunctions of our world. One of these is a rampant, hyperconsumerism. Our global consumption patterns are a hamster wheel of action Paul Ginsborg summarizes as "desire-acquisition-use-disillusionment-discarding-desire again."[2] It is the choice to discard God's "economy" of love, nourishment, and relationships for an economy of addictive consumption. It is building up storehouses of overripe and rancid fruit, cutting down trees, and an addiction that serves as a god in an otherwise godless society. It is defining ourselves not as God's people within God's world but as whatever stamp is on our next box of acquisitions or as the hero of our own story. Instead of living in God's garden world, we are posting our own pictures on the garden gate.

The Fall Revisited

Hyperconsumerism

What defines you? Your education? Your profession? Your race? Your sexuality? Your first language? Your preferred cuisine? In this culture, you are most clearly defined by your pecking place in the economic order. Of course, this is nothing new. At the end of the fourteenth century, the Dominican preacher John Bromyard wrote this about lawyers: "Advocates would be more truthful if they began their presentations not with 'In the name of God, Amen,' but rather with 'In the name of hard cash, Amen.'"[3]

More than ever before in history, this is the greatest and most important of all the secular economic commandments of civil religion: "Thou shalt consume." It is the one commandment we are piously obeying.

The dominant culture of our day is consumer culture. In fact, for at least half a century, being a consumer has trumped being a citizen in Western societies. The conquering power of the American imperium in the twentieth century was not a military accomplishment of tanks and troops but a consumerist triumph of autos, sneakers, and fast foods. Now the Asian imperium is poised to conquer the twenty-first century in the same way.[4]

In a consumer society there are inevitably two kinds of slaves: prisoners of addiction and prisoners of envy.

—Ivan Illich, *Tools for Conviviality*

But consumerism is a boring, tired, squalid creed, uninspired and uninspiring. Human life is bottoming out on consumerism's top-drawer druthers, top-floor ladders, and bottom-line scorecards. And "the sweet life" is not one with enough stocks and bonds to buy whatever you want. In fact, the stocks and bonds of wealth can place the wealthy in stocks and bonds as surely as judges and juries did in colonial times. There are more people living behind bars than are behind bars. There are more of God's people suffering from emotional and spiritual "gold" bars built up from our own consumption and addictions than there are people languishing behind bars in any of the physical prisons of our rehabilitation institutions. Our drive to consume is consuming us. We have created our own "debtors' prisons."

The "houses" we build for ourselves can consume our own humanity, as well as our world. Only God's household economy promotes domestic tranquility and creativity. Like the burning bush, God's *oikonomia* never consumes but only burns with a passion and energy that can sustain us through every peril and problem in life.

Wealth itself is not the culprit. The wealthy and poor alike are in need of Jesus's mercy and salvation. In fact, when Jesus died, the wealthy as well as the poor were on his lips: "the wealthy will be filled with good things," he said; "the poor shall eat and be satisfied. The rich of the earth will eat and worship."[5] Only when wealth and materiality become idols of worship and fixation instead of icons for sacrifice and ministry will the wealthy abandon God. Even the poor can harbor empty addictions or gods of consumption or priorities over relationships with God and neighbor—"all have sinned and fall short of the glory of God."[6]

War and Strife

Too much of the antiglobalization movement is a hatred of the rich—rich people, rich nations, rich diets—by people who are often relatively rich. It is easy for the rich to have a cultivated distaste for money. As *The Simpsons's* Mr. Burns puts it, money is for the poor. That is why the rich often travel with no money on them. The rich are the ones who romanticize the poor, even confusing poverty with poetry. Not the poor.

In the Bible, there is no sense of a war of poverty, nor is there a sense of any war on the rich. Jeremiah attacks the faith of both poor and rich,[7] and Isaiah consigns both rich and poor to the judgment of Yahweh for the same reasons.[8] Proverbs warns about the dangers of self-confidence, not the rejection of wealth.[9] Wealth is not bad in itself, but wealth comes with slippery ramps to pride and blasphemy, especially the deceit that, as we tell ourselves, "My power and the might of my own hand have gotten me this wealth,"[10] or the delusion that, if you like something, you are entitled to it because, as the advertisers say, "You're worth it." It is not true that the poorer you are, the more Jesus will love you.

To say "blessed are the poor" is not to say "cursed are the rich." The kingdom of God is blessedness for all, the breaking of all barriers between God and God's creatures and the lowering of the drawbridge of God's castle to all castes and classes. Jesus reached out to both and loved both at the same time. Jesus had middle-class friends (Mary, Martha, Lazarus), middle-class disciples (Peter, Andrew), rich friends (Lydia, Joanna [wife of Chuza], Herod's business manager Susanna),[11] a rich disciple (Matthew), and lots of poor friends.

In fact, to be against the rich is to be against one of the heroes of one of Jesus's greatest parables, the Good Samaritan, who was also the Good, Rich Samaritan. The rich Zaccheus, up the tree, had to "come down." The poor, the beggar at the Bethesda pool, had to "stand up." Jesus reached out to both, but in different ways. The materially poor can be spiritually rich, and they can be spiritually poor; the materially rich can be spiritually poor, and they can be spiritually rich.

If the rich could hire other people to die for them the poor
would make a wonderful living.

—old Yiddish riddle[12]

The collapse of the Western Roman Empire led to a period of human history mistakenly called the Dark Ages. When you see the incredible art and jewelry that was produced, the stained glass masterpieces, and the Gothic cathedrals with all their artwork and stone carvings, you say, "How can this be?" The Dark Ages were never "dark." But what made them so barbaric and dismal was that only the wealthy, and that meant only a very few royal families and churches, could invest their time and resources in creative pursuits. The masses of humanity worked like slaves, round the clock in horrid conditions, to eke out an existence in a very short life.

In some ways, wealth creation is not what endangers the finer things of life, including finer feelings and finer thoughts. Wealth is what enables culture and art, the possibility of having finer things, finer feelings, and finer thoughts. Anyone who has ever studied preindustrial societies realizes that far from capitalism destroying community, undermining friendship, and soiling love, capitalism gives people resources, especially time, which increases human freedom to form communities, cultivate friendships, fall in love, create art, and think deep thoughts. Whether we choose to spend our wealth in these ways is another matter.

Walls and Barriers

The question is not what side is God on—the rich or the poor? The question is whether we're on God's side, breaking down those barriers that separate the two and keep them from reconceiving each other in light of each other. Jesus scandalized the "love the rich" religious culture of his day by telling "love the poor" stories ("Dives and Lazarus"). Jesus scandalizes the "hate the rich" religious culture of our day by telling "love the rich" stories ("The

Good Samaritan"). Sometimes it seems as if Jesus wrote the handbook on "How to Make Everyone, Everywhere, Mad at You."

In Christ, there is neither Jew nor Gentile, male nor female, rich nor poor. Jesus never so much as treated everyone the "same" as never treated anyone the same way, rich or poor. The Rich Young Ruler was asked to sell all. Zaccheus was not. The "Zaccheus 50-50 Principle" is give away as much as you keep.

E. Stanley Jones visited Russia in the 1930s. Upon returning to the States, he wrote a book on his experience entitled "Christ's Alternative to Communism." The outline of the book is based on Luke 4:18-19, which is a quotation of Jesus from Isaiah 61:1-3. The "alternative" Christ provides is a new social gospel, Jones said, which is

1. good news to the economically disinherited

2. good news to the socially and politically disinherited

3. good news to the physically disinherited

4. good news to the morally and spiritually disinherited

One day, the current order will give way to an order where, in Jones's words, "two things remain: a kingdom, which I believe is the ultimate order, and a person, who I believe is the ultimate person."[13] But until then, the call to be human in a new social gospel is the call of the incarnation to be flesh to the stranger, to be blood to the neighbor, to be bone to the homeless, whether rich or poor, insider or outsider.

Above all and in all and through all is the holy will,
the creative purpose, of the Most High.
The world is God's and He made it.
The confusions of history are in the grasp of His manifold wisdom.
God overrules and works through the purposes of people,
bringing to naught their stubborn and rebellious lust for power,
but building their fidelity into the structure of His reign upon earth.

—from the Tambaram Confession, drawn up in Malay, 1938

The best kept secret of the rich? That having everything is closer to having nothing than anyone could imagine. Money soothes the nerves, but an over-dose can strain the strands that tie and bind us together. The allure of wealth can lure us from our calling in the most stealthy and unassuming ways. There is a saying that "you are what you do." If your "all in all" is wealth, your identity is found in your economic status, which becomes more important than either Me or We.

Do you have "attachment anxiety" when you are away from the shopping mall? Do you fear the loss of your storehouses of things? At antique auctions, a smart bidder on a piece of furniture or something that catches the eye is always willing to let the item go. The danger comes when you love it so much, you cannot let it go. As Max Weber put it in classic form: "In [Puritan Richard] Baxter's view, the care for external goods should only lie on the shoulders of the 'saint like a light cloak, which can be thrown aside at any moment.' But fate decreed that the cloak should become an iron cage."[14]

All of our treasures must be willing sacrifices on the altar that never jeopardize our "House and Garden" relationship with God and others. We are called to love God first, neighbor second, and all of the created world. We are called to serve God in all of it. When we make money and possessions our first love and primary focus, all of our energy goes into protecting, hoarding, and attaining both that money and our own interests. And we live in a culture that tells us we should put our own interests first. But hoarding is like building up toxins in our body. Sooner or later, we find our lives poisoned and sick.

I once knew a family whose every possession was lost in a fire. They lost every "thing," but every family member survived. When they celebrated Christmas only a week later, they were filled with joy and the spirit of love. They lost all their possessions, their house, and their money, but they had each other, the most precious treasures of life. They said it was the best Christmas they had ever had.

John Perry Barlow, cofounder of the Electronic Freedom Foundation and one-time lyricist for the Grateful Dead, asked a PopTech audience whether they would give up all of their material things or all of their relationships if they were forced to choose. Which way would they go? Everyone in the room chose their relationships. When asked why, someone said, "I can always replace my possessions. But I can never replace my relationships, and without those relationships, I can never hope to replace my possessions."

Yet there are people who, when the stock market fell, plummeted along with it to their death in suicide jumps. Those who, when faced with losing houses and riches or when faced with a lifetime of hard work, fell into a life of alcoholism and despair. This despair does not come from the loss of materiality but the loss of identity. Consumerism equates acquisition of possessions with an identity as an acquisitionist. In its very nature, acquisition does not build identity, it tears it down. The quest for more and more, whether as therapy or metaphysical activity, has left us without a sense of identity.[15] As in any addiction, consumerism eats away identity from the inside out. Is it any wonder, as Southern novelist/semiotician Walker Percy used to put it, "We don't coincide with ourselves."[16]

Where does your identity lie? Are you living in your own skin? Are you living the "sweet life" or the saccharine life, or perhaps a shopaholic life? The most important determinant of the sweet life is not the extrinsic quantity of your possessions but the intrinsic quality of your relationships with God, with others, with yourself, and with creation. Only when your identity is rooted in God can you remain stable in a world of consumerist storms and materialist temptations. Freedom is less about physical location than about Jesus's location—is he on the inside looking out, or on the outside looking in? The problem is that, as the eighteenth-century philosopher Adam Ferguson warned, our commitment to one another becomes less and less as our material wealth increases. This is why another eighteenth-century theologian, John Wesley, warned about the dangers of riches while himself being rich:

> I fear, whenever riches have increased the essence of religion has decreased in the same proportion. Therefore I do not see how it is possible, in the nature of things, for any revival of true religion to continue long. But as riches increase, so will pride, anger, and love of the world in all its branches. . . . So although the form of religion remains, the spirit is swiftly vanishing away. Is there no way to prevent this—this continual decay of pure religion.[17]

Living East of Eden

There are crimes of the body, crimes of the mind, and crimes of the soul. In a way, consumerism is a crime of all three, funded by plastic coinage,[18] fueled by plastered courage, and sexualized by a plethora of *Playboy* philosophies.[19] A Me/We whole gospel cannot be lived under the criminal spell of (in the stocks and bonds of) consumerism. Jesus is the cure for consumerism.

Discipleship formation is increasing the soul's bandwidth to perceive, receive, and conceive Jesus.

Up until the eighteenth century, the verb *to consume* was uniformly negative. Only in the mid-eighteenth century did the verb become morally neutral, associated with the use of objects. Previously it was associated with waste and destruction: to "destroy by or like fire or disease; to cause to vanish." Alas, that is what consumerism is doing to our lives, our churches, our planet: destroying our human habitat, and our relationships with God and with one another.

God's "economy" of relationships is grounded in Jesus. When we put God first, relationships and connections first, we forge an economy of "House and Garden" that is less Babel and more beautiful, satisfying, filling, joyful, and eco-nomical. *Eco* in French comes from the Greek word meaning "house." Your economy is the way you "manage your house." Or better said, the way we manage *God's* house.

When God is sovereign, and we are the "keepers" of the household, the way we "till and keep" our houses (God's garden world) reveals either an economy of love and grace, creativity and abundance in the relational covenant life of Jesus, or an economy of selfishness, "equality," our own justice, and an accumulation of "things" that neither satisfy nor salve the soul.

How do we as Christians, as the church, bring the gospel into this native culture with integrity, not merely condemning the culture we are in but not condoning it either?[20] How do we forge a creative economy while not falling prey to the perils of JDD (Jesus Deficit Disorder) consumerism?

There is nothing wrong with consumption: Only God doesn't need to consume. We have to consume oxygen to live. To live is to consume—air, food, water, love. Life must live on life, both in the natural world, where we consume plant and animal life daily, and in the holy consumption of the sacred world, where we feed on divine life to live eternally.

Likewise, there is nothing wrong with collecting. We are all collectors: we collect our thoughts; we collect ourselves before going on stage; we want to appear calm and collected. We even collect "things," as Samuel Johnson noted himself about collecting "sermons" in 1781: "in all collections [of sermons], Sir, the desire of augmenting it grows stronger in proportion to the advance in acquisition; as motion is accelerated by the continuance of the impetus."[21]

But when we live to collect, when we live to consume, not consume to live, that's called consumerism. Consumerism robs our souls of their essential grandness and eternal weight, rendering them vaporish and vapid. We have created a world with one-third too much debt. Wonder how that happened? "I consume, therefore I am." In our all-consuming ways, we are not just consumers of things but of each other. We treat each other not as an image of God but as just another consumable. In market relationships, everything is commercialized, and everyone has a price; economic transactions are everywhere, and valuations (or devaluations) of people are made at the drop of a hat.

We Are All Consumers

Living honestly in a consumer culture means recognizing, first of all, that we are all consumers. It is impossible to live today and not be a "consumer" unless you return to a barter, off-the-grid, back-to-the-land mode of living, or delude yourself into a gnostic existence. Technology and peer communities are empowering collaborative-consumption—sharing, lending, trading, renting, gifting, and swapping.[22] But any way you approach it, you will need to shop for some things—even if those things are what you'll need to get off and stay off the grid, or to keep your gnostic delusion going. Opposing shopping is like opposing globalization: The opposition doesn't solve the problem.

Second, no consumer wants to "consume." Consumers want to love and be loved. "I shop therefore I am" makes you what? A shopper? Only those "Real Housewives of Beverly Hills" want the identity of "shopper." The only thing worse than to be defined by stuff is to be defined by death—the death of a relationship, the death of a spouse, the death of a dream.

Instead of a disdain for shopping, let's create new forms of shopping that conceive rather than consume.

What's wrong with the current global economic system is not consumption but consumerism, this organizing principle of life whereby we are what we buy, commodities replace communities, the good becomes another goodie, and enough is never enough. Consumerism is deep in our gene pool. The first consumerists were Adam and Eve, guilty of a forbidden consumption, the needless consuming of a sacred fruit, for whom enough was "not enough." Commanded to "Eat freely" of every tree in the garden, except one, Adam and Eve had to consume it all. All but one wasn't enough. The arrogant need to "have it all" is the essence of the fall.

President Dwight D. Eisenhower was only the first in a long line of presidents who, when things got tough, told us be tough by going shopping. "It is a duty of every American to consume," he said when the economy was slowing down. Our social duty in our "religion of materialism" is to do as we are told and go shopping.[23] Look around you. We did. We shopped till we dropped. Whole economies have fallen. We're shopped out, and our children and grandchildren are left picking up the droppings of our shoppy life and bling-bling pleasures. Our consumerist pursuit of stuff and security (financial, physical, personal) puts us away in padded cells for the sane. We can't keep going like this.

But Christians aren't anti-things or antimaterialistic. The centerpiece doctrine of the incarnation is an affirmation of the material world. People need to finger relics, leavings, fixtures, fittings, especially in a cyberspace, virtual-reality culture. A story transforms a thing into a relic. When you give a story to an artifact, it turns into an icon. A right relationship with our things does not mean we worship consumer goods, or entrust our security to possessions—or power, wealth, weapons, the upper hand—or promise us a meaningful identity based on consumption. A right relationship with our things brings out the sacredness of our world, a world where people are subjects, not objects, and our things serve, not rule over, our lives. Our culture today is a culture that objectifies everything and everyone.

Go to a hospital, and you're not a patient, you're a "customer." Get on a plane, and you're not a passenger, you're a "customer." Go to a restaurant, and you're not a hungry person, you're a "customer." Go to college, and you're not a student, you're a "customer." We even shop online for a wife or husband, or a church, the same way we shop for a lawnmower.

The issue is not the amount of our spending. The issue is the account of our spending. Too much of our spending goes by the name of *Chindogu* spending—a Japanese word for all the useless things we tend to buy.[24] Perhaps the category of "People and Things" should really be changed to "Things and Things," or rather "Things and People who have become Things," in Arcimboldo-style fashion where humans are made of "stuff."

The Church of England approved a prayerbook for the third millennium called "New Start Worship." The faithful are advised, in a striking paragraph, that

> where we shop, how we shop and what we buy is a living statement of what we believe. . . . Shopping which involves the shopper in making ethical and religious judgments may be nearer to the worship God requires than

98

any number of pious prayers in church. . . . If we take our roles as God's stewards seriously, shoppers collectively are a very powerful group. . . . If, when we ourselves are not on the poverty line, we always go for the cheapest price, without considering that this price is achieved through ethically unacceptable working conditions somewhere in the world, we are making a statement about our understanding of the word neighbor.[25]

Called to Be Servants

As God's people, we are caretakers and vineyard servants not of just the earth but in a covenant relationship with God that affects all of our behavior. God's economy is not an economy of materialism but of love, meaning, relationships, grace, and dignity. We need not to be shoppers who love things and live to shop but people who love God and life who shop to live and serve.

The salary of the chief executive of the large corporation is not a market reward for achievement. It is frequently in the nature of a warm personal gesture by the individual to himself.

—John Kenneth Galbraith, *Annals of an Abiding Liberal*

Homo Consumens

One of the greatest failures of the church in the past fifty years has been its inability to provide a culture of consumption with an alternative model. If truth be told, much of the church has so bought into a consumption culture that if Karl Marx were alive today, he would not accuse religion of being the "opiate" of the people but an ornament of conspicuous consumption. He came close with his dictum: "Accumulate, accumulate: this is the law and the prophets."

Consumerism is the new civil religion, indeed the first global civil religion and the number one religion in the world, especially when it combines with a techno-fix faith. It has its own consumption creed, consumption rituals (Black Friday, Cyber Monday), consumption pledge, consumption gods (celebrities), consumption cathedrals (malls), and consumption polls (vote at check-out). The consumption of brands, visual logos, and celebrity magazines has conspired to create a surrogate spirituality that is now arguably the closest global competitor to Christianity. Consumption is the greatest social-control vehicle ever concocted by the human species.

The market has become a god, and consumption a religion. We refer to the market as though it were a living being—the market is "nervous" or "happy" or "skeptical" or "uncertain." We anxiously await the market god's verdict on our behavior like our ancestors feared God's judgment on their actions.[26] In Babylon, the anti-God city, everything is based on the market, and "marketolatry" is enforced in every walk of life. Everything *is* a market. Even people are a commodity. That's what the mark of the beast is about:[27] a world where you can't buy or sell without selling out, a world where the wheel of fortune is a circle of hell.

The dominant religion of our time is economism. . . .
Virtue is called competition, and vice is inefficiency.
Salvation comes through shopping alone.

—John Cobb, *Matters of Life and Death*

The church has proven to be as prone as the culture to confuse a creditable history with a credit history. We can be as consumeristic about spiritual things as physical things: we collect experiences, collect meditative techniques, collect special powers and gifts, collect gurus (aka "leaders"), and collect sacred objects and pilgrimages (conferences). The church's attractional consumerist message of "Come to church and we'll meet your needs" is no different than the culture's message that bombards us daily in 3,500 sermons (a.k.a. ads) that all say one thing: "You're a god;" "You're number one;" "You deserve *more*."

My friend Rich Melheim likes to tell of the 872-day siege of Leningrad (from 1941 to 1944), when the city elders had a difficult decision to make. The Nazis had cut off most supply routes to the city. The few remaining truck routes across the frozen lake were being bombed daily. By the fall of 1941, it became clear there was only one-third the amount of grain needed to get the city through the winter. By November, 350 people were dying daily. By December, 1,600 corpses were turning up on the streets each day.

What would the elders do? Would they cordon off two-thirds of the city and feed only one-third? They couldn't bear to make that decision, so instead they mixed their bread with anything they could find—sawdust, cottonseed, cellulose, and manure. That winter, hundreds of thousands of children went to bed starving to death on bloated stomachs. When the siege finally lifted, somewhere between 635,000 and one million Russians had perished in that city alone.

Most parents want the best for their children. But what are we feeding them in a consumer culture? Sawdust and manure.

Our consumer ideology floats around in our subconscious and infiltrates everything, including our theology and worship, even making innocent "hunger" language (e.g., "the heart hungers") treacherous, as it feeds our human needs-orientation. The innocuous idea of "being fed" because we are "hungry" becomes quickly consumerist, meet-my-needs ideology. Jesus doesn't feed us with the comfort foods we crave but with the living water we need that leads to health and holiness.

We in our consumerist churches spend money and time building Babel towers to try to get to a "feel good" place to call our own. We create our own personal "heaven," and woe to anyone who disrupts "our" church. We have in our current century's market idolatry created a "whore of Babylon" of our own making. And the question of the day is, is the bride of Christ only there for the "food"?

The empire of goods has become the empire of our gods. But value cannot be the price of goods we buy. Value must be the price of sacrifices we invest in the good, the true, and the beautiful.[28] Our premodern ancestors did not automatically applaud something because it brought economic benefit. At least until the Renaissance, people filtered every "advance" through relational and ethical grids before calculating and celebrating their economic effects. Biblical economics means something very different from our consumerist economy. God is invested in an economy of covenant living.

Incarnating Christ in the Church and Community

So how do we incarnate Christ within a consumer culture? We start by incarnating Christ within a Christian culture, one that spreads and grows with a renewed passion for evangelism and salvation of people and world, a renewed faith in the power of Jesus to resurrect and renew, and an example of a people who demonstrate a God-first culture of humility and service within the body of Christ that is the church. What does it look like when people with a God identity cultivate and keep God's economy? What does it mean for the world to be "God owned" not human built? How does a Me/We identity with God bear creative fruit in an economy of love that can spread throughout a world?

God Owned, Not Human Built

First, we need to move beyond the sloganeering ideology of scarcity, as in "Live More Simply So That Others May Simply Live." The busier we get, the more we fetishize the simple life. But God governs the world from a position of abundance, not scarcity. In the words of the psalmist, "You brought us out into a place that's wide, . . . a place that's wealthy."[29]

And out of that abundance we are promised more than anything we could ask or think, far beyond anything we could deserve or desire. The ideal society of the future is not today's Cuba, or one without the "luxury" of pets, in spite of what the Worldwatch Institute says.[30] God's abundance comes from the inside out, from the Me to the We. God's economy is an economy of grace that isn't grounded in simplicity of life but in simplicity of faith. Simplicity has become a religion. But is there a "simple" route or recipe to Bolognese? A "simple" way to Béarnaise sauce? A "simple" way to being in relationship? Besides, that motto of "Live Simple" has already been tried and found unenforceable at best, so much "sustainababble" at worst.[31] Simplicity didn't work for Mao Zedong, who imposed a similar slogan on his people and enforced an ideology of "involuntary simplicity." Mao insisted that as far as material consumption was concerned, the bicycle, the radio, the wristwatch and the sewing machine were the only possessions necessary.[32]Anyone who has been to China in the past decade can testify to how well the ideology of diminished dreams inherent in "involuntary simplicity" or even "voluntary simplicity" is playing itself out.[33]

The comrades must be taught to remain modest, prudent, and free from arrogance and rashness in their style of work. The comrades must be taught to preserve the style of plain living and hard struggle.

—Mao Tse-tung

Second, we must resist the temptation to build just one more "system" or yet another legalistic, governmental, sanctioning institution that enforces an order based on a governmental moral or justice code. Or to try to "save" the system we are in. This was the chief error of the first social gospel movement.

A Me/We economy is an economy that lives out of the abundance of God's grace and the creativity of our humanness. It begins relationally and ends relationally, moves in step with grace and humility, accepts personal responsibility, and is immersed with an awareness of wholeness and connectivity. It innovates and dreams. It expands and gives. Above all, it "tills and keeps" a covenant as old as the hills. Or as I prefer to put it, it conserves and conceives.

Conserve and Conceive

Holiness Living

Where consumerism feeds on objectification of life and world, conception celebrates and delights in the human spirit. And it attributes its delight to God's Spirit. In a sense, it is holiness living with practical implications. When we conserve God's covenant, we cultivate that relationship in our lives. And then we conceive that relationship within everything we say and do. An economy of conception is based in a conserve-and-conceive paradigm. Without conserving the relationships that nurture and sustain us and our world, we cannot conceive. Without conceiving, we have no purpose to our conservation. So what does it mean to conserve and conceive?

The only way to rise towards God, following the example of our divine master, is to create.

—Paul Gauguin

Living as Art

The Alexandrian synagogue called God *patēr kai poietes*, "father and maker" or "father and author." Our Greco-Jewish forebears in the earliest churches saw Jesus as the *poiesis* (storyline or poem) of that poietic Father.

Whatever your theology, wherever you're coming from, God is defined in terms of creativity. The spark of creativity is the sparkle of divinity. Life in Christ *is* art. Every one of us is an original creation, God's outdoor art. One day we'll end up in the Ultimate Gallery.

The first "word" of Creator God is creative: "Let there be light."[34] God's essence is Creator, and creativity is what God does, not out of need but out of love. God enjoyed God's own creativity: "God saw everything that he had made, and indeed, it was very good."[35] But then our Ur-Story, or Urstory, zooms in on one creature of that "very good" creation, and God issues a Prime Directive, a divine directive, to "tend and keep," or as I like to call it, "conserve and conceive": conserve God's creative identity in our current relationships and conceive God's creativity in new relationships. It starts with Me and moves to We.

Created in the image of God, humans are called to collaborate with the divine in the unfinished symphony of creation.[36] There are some masterpieces that may be designed not to be finished. Like Schubert's "Unfinished Symphony," like James Joyce's *Ulysses*, which has never been finished by any reader, no matter what he or she says. Like creation. A continuum of human creativity and divine action is established in Genesis, a participation in the created order known in the Hebrew tradition as TIKKUN OLAM, the Midrashic Rabbis' view of human responsibility in the covenantal relationship. Each one of us has been gifted with creative power.

So throw out all spoiled virtue and cancerous evil in the garbage.
In simple humility, let our gardener, God, landscape you
with the Word, making a salvation-garden of your life.

—James 1:21-22 *"The Message"*

We conserve and conceive the primal relationship with God and keep God in everything throughout all generations. Creativity is conceived through relationality, combining the unrelated into new relationships. God's creation or God's relationship with us (garden relationship is a metaphor) is the medium for the relationships and creativity of every sustained and perpetuated relationship.

Garden Living

God conceived a garden in which to play. *Garden* is the same word in Hebrew, Persian, Arabic, and Greek, and means "paradise." So God created a paradise planet in the Milky Way Galaxy, planet Earth, the garden of God. God created humans not just to take care of the garden (conserve) but to make our joy and reflection and praise of God more pervasively beautiful and marvelous (conceive). We become spreaders and generators of beauty, truth, and goodness. Humans are gardeners of the galaxy, gardeners of our relationship with God, of this garden planet Earth, and all of our relationships in it, which we are to plenish for God's good pleasure. And we are also gardeners of our souls. If every garden is a form of autobiography, God's garden is God's autobiography.

God's garden is the relational "soil" in which we and God commune. Relational space. And we are imbued or incarnated with Christ's Spirit of creativity. As image-makers, our calling is to create everything with God's *oikonomia* label. We may be the hired help, the subcontractors, but Jesus is the Master Architect and Builder.

We conserve God's creativity by continuing to conceive that divine creativity, not by humans going off on their own creative binges, as some have done like Joseph Mengele, Osama bin Laden, Elisabeth Bathory, Heinrich Himmler, Nero, Atilla the Hun, Mao Zedong, Genghis Kahn, Pol Pot (to pick some obvious names). Artist Adolf Hitler was one of the most "creative" people who ever lived. But what he conceived was anything but God designed. But we conceive as Christians through communion with Christ, from which all creativity in us emerges passionately and powerfully. Creativity in the church means allowing God to create in and through the Me and the We.

Not Cocreators

Some theologians use the language of "cocreator," but it's a dangerous metaphor. In the language of the old bumper sticker, "If God is your copilot, someone is in the wrong seat." I prefer the language of subcreators or subcontractors to describe our status conveyed in the command to continue God's creativity. *Cocreation* is playing God. *Subcreation* is acknowledging that there is a Godprint on everything we create—God's signature in all of it. God's image is to be our imagination. Designed by God, the world mirrors the divine.

God creates and I assemble what has already been created.
—George Balanchine[37]

Sent as God's Ambassadors

As creators, our activity is akin to that of God. But we were not created to be God's successors but God's ambassadors, God's own image, "children of the Most High."[38] The desires and designs are God's, not ours. We aren't starting up something. We are joining and catalyzing, "as above, so below."

That's why the Hebrews ordered the day around the evening, rather than the morning. Not just the Sabbath day but every day begins at sundown and ends at sundown. God's creativity starts in the evening, when we are sleeping. We rise in the morning to join what God is already doing. We awaken to join God's active creativity. In fact, physicists tell us that our universe is so fecund, so continuously creative, more a multiverse of invisible parallel worlds than a universe of one visible world, that each moment is a new moment of creation, and each creation reshuffles physics.[39] Life is a series of big-bang shifts, whether the sound uttered is a big bang or a baby whimper, a wow, or a whisper.

Preserve and create are our rival verbs at the dawn of this new century.
—Carlos Fuentes, "Urbanities"

When Adam "named" creation, he was not viewing things and then "naming" them. Rather, by naming them, Adam was calling things into being,[40] continuing God's creativity by speaking ("And God said"), and thus calling the world into big-bang being ("let there be light"). In naming the animals, Adam was conceiving a voice for each of them. Adam's first act was to conserve and conceive.

Bringing Voice to the Silent

We are also called to conceive God's voice in the world. God created the world with divine voice, and all the world came into being, became visual

106

in living color. Whenever we as disciples conceive God's voice in the world, we give voice to the silent and make visible the unseen, all those whom society has given no face and no voice. Whenever we recognize someone in need, whenever we hear someone's plea, we are conceiving voices for all God's people. To make audible the pain of the desperate of the world, so that they may be heard, and so they may be seen, is a conserve-and-conceive economy of love.

Conserving and conceiving, consolidation and innovation, tradition and revolution, continuity and change are the creative dynamics of human life. In his essay "The Conservative," Ralph Waldo Emerson wrote: "Conservatism makes no poetry, breathes no prayer, has no invention; it is all memory. Reform has no gratitude, no prudence, no husbandry. . . . Each is a good half, but an impossible whole."[41] A whole gospel embraces both the careful conservationist and the creative artist.

The New Creation

The garden of Eden was designed to be a conserver society and a conceiver society. The human spirit is meant to be artistic in style, even wild/untamed in appearance, but conservationist at heart. A gospel of Me/We embraces both conserving and conceiving. It eradicates divisions; conserves wholeness; fizzes with creative ideas; generates goodness, beauty, truth; and dreams the future.

What does this look like in the church? In the world? At the very least, churches should be philanthropic powerhouses of love and grace, economies of relationality that raise up and resource constructive alternatives to consumerist cultures. Too often the primary focus of churches has been consumerist itself—the ABCs of attendance, buildings, and cash—or a dragging of the church through the MBA diploma mill and its metrics of butts, buildings, budgets, not on spreading the gospel economy of amazing grace and abundant life.

Asking today's Christians to live more abundantly in Christ is much like asking an urbanite to live off the land and farm for a living. What would living differently mean—off the land and off the grid? In a culture that no longer is in touch with the land, "living from the land" is a foreign concept. In a church culture that is saturated with consumerism, what does living in covenant with God mean? What does it look like? Off-the-grid living doesn't have to be outside electric power grids but outside of materialism's grip and grind. Whereas a consumer economy results in gridlocked living, a conceiver economy cultivates off-the-grid creativity and giving.

What does your budget look like? God first? We first? Or Me first? Many of our churches spend all their time and resources to build ivory palaces, rather than enabling others to see Calvary. Jesus, the Son of God, didn't need a palace to be born in then. And he doesn't need one today. He just needs open and consecrated hearts.

Yet, there is no We without Me. In order for the We to function as a conceiver economy, there must be a deep discipleship that is committed to personating Jesus in the world. You cannot function as a body without each part coordinating in its own unique way. The We cannot work without the Me.

Today, we know that bodily illnesses are all connected. If you have a disease, it can come from an imbalance in your gut or in your blood or in deficiencies in your body. Something on your skin may issue from an imbalance in your colon. A pain in your leg could telegraph a problem in your spine. When one part of the body malfunctions, it trips the rest. This is what the Apostle Paul knew about the community of the church. Personal responsibility and commitment to the whole of the body is paramount to the entire body's health.

Whereas in a planned economy there is an overarching legalism regulating the roles of these parts, in an organic body like the church Christ moves and guides and anoints what each part does within that body. And Christ is incarnated within each part, as well as directing the body as the head. When the system is in control, the body becomes victim to a mechanism. When Christ is in control and the body is being re-formed by the Spirit into wholeness and harmony, the body remains organic, living, growing, healthy. A Me/We gospel is a salvation gospel.

Living out of a place of salvation is living in health and mind-body-spirit wholeness. Our churches and our communities don't have an economic problem so much as a faith problem. We feel we need to build our own houses because we don't trust the power of the Spirit. We don't trust God's creativity. We would rather usurp God's place and worship our own "creativity." This is the Babelian (and Babylon) lifestyle that travels the way in "angel gear." "Angel gear" is New Zealand–lorry driverese for coming down from the mountains with engine off and no brakes. How many people go through life in angel gear—no brakes, inertia driven, and no powering of the Spirit? A Me/We life is Spirit-powered and faith-braked.

108

> *The only message at the moment is money, success, power and it's like a Big Mac;*
> *you're told to eat it, but afterwards you're still empty.*
>
> —Preacher John in the British play "13" by Mike Bartlett

In fact, even if we do give credit to God, we like to believe we are co-creators with God. The First Commandment ("tend and till the garden" or as I translate it, "conserve and conceive") calls us to continue to create, not as "co-creators" but as subcontractors. Jesus said: "My father has never yet ceased his creativity, and I am creating too."[42] To follow Jesus means to participate with him in God's continual creative activity. It's time to trust God's creative spirit to surprise us with new manifestations of what God can do here on planet Earth. Or as I pray, "Lord, not my blueprint to follow, but your blue sky to dream."[43]

A creative "conceiver" economics is grounded in what we make sacred, what we put first. A Me/We economics is a sacred and sacrificial economics, a creative economics, an economy of abundant grace. It is an economics based in personal responsibility, each person a subcreator in God's "House and Garden" world. It is an economics based not in statements or systems but in a savior. The only thing that makes the market hospitable to the human spirit is social capital, an imposed moral logic on the market that is embedded in a Me/We life built around generosity, sacrifice, loyalty, forgiveness. None of these are virtues of capitalism. But they are all virtues of a conceiver capital and conceiver market that blesses the future, and doesn't curse it.

Conserve and conceive. These work together to make a garden world and a Me/We economy.

No Conceiving without Conserving

God is first a conservationist. God is "not the abstract creator, but he who caresses the daily and nightly earth,"[44] in the words of one of the greatest poets of the twentieth-century (Irish poet/novelist Patrick Kavanagh). Jesus valued nature as more than a resource, and nowhere in the Bible does the "sanctity of human life" mean the insanctity of other forms of life and other species.

A Me/We whole gospel conserves even as it conceives. Conservation is primary and preliminary to conception. Conserving what already exists is more important than innovation, continuity more important than change, advent more elemental than invent, the renaturing of everyday life more significant than the technologizing of everyday life.

Conserving God's covenant means being in a relationship of knowing God and one another, of knowing the earth in an intimate and caring way, and to be in a relationship of holiness with God, neighbor, ourselves, and our world. It means keeping the covenant real by remembering God in everyday things. We cannot do the work of bearing (conceiving) something new until we do the due diligence of knowing who we are (conserving).

In conceiving, we are invited into fruitbearing. Prayer is what brings fire and fruit to our faith. In conserving, we are entrusted with relationships wherein we cultivate the divine presence within our humanness, so that these relationships bear fruit.

"There was yet no human to till the soil . . ."
No human, no blooming.

—Leonard Sweet

Just as the Hebrews took care to sustain their land for future abundance, we are called to an interdependency with the earth and everyone in it, to keep all of our relationships fertile and fresh, to prepare and repair for God's habitation. In our conserving, we also teach our children about the grace of God, to cherish "the ground from which we came," even as we remove the thorns, thistles, and weeds that choke love and threaten life.

We have come to view ourselves, in the words of René Descartes, as "masters and possessors of the earth."[45] Nature is increasingly commercialized, something to be conquered and consumed. We consume and discard "almost in one motion," observes dancer Twyla Tharp.[46] The species known as homo sapiens has become "homo rapiens,"[47] turning water and air, the fluids of life, into our garbage cans.[48] Half of all hospital patients in the developing world suffer from water-related diseases. One hundred million tons of plastic is produced every year, 10 percent of which ends up in the ocean, killing birds, fish, and so on. Our ancestors used to be able to say, "There are as many fish in the sea as ever came out of it." No more. Fish and animal species are only being preserved by arks called zoos.

At the same time we need to unhook ourselves from electronic umbilicals and get outside, away from our privatized lifestyles and screen-saver soteriologies dominated by the blue screen of death and the blue line of hyperheaven, the out-of-doors is becoming more and more dangerous. The rays of the blazing sun, once the source of life and vitamin D, are now the source of cancer and God knows what else through our ozone-depleted, carbon-crammed atmosphere. Making matters even worse, the amount of sunlight reaching the earth has been decreasing 2 to 3 percent each decade since the 1950s, and more in some areas such as Hong Kong, where sunlight decreased by 37 percent in the past fifty years. As anyone who has been to Beijing or Seoul can tell you, soot particles big enough to bite bounce the sunlight back into outer space, keeping the sun out and dimming the planet as it forces us to wear facemasks to breathe.

What falls from the rich man's table is not crumbs, but poisons and plastics.

—John V. Taylor, *Enough Is Enough*

The biblical narrative provides us with more of a framework for the care of creation than any other alternatives now being prescribed. From day one, biblical faith serves and conserves gardens, reconnecting humans to the natural world, "the moon and the stars, which You have ordained."[49] The Nobel laureate and Polish poet Czeslaw Milosz gave as the best definition of communism as the "enemy of orchards."[50] The Bible might be defined as the "friend of orchards." Or as one Hebrew song voices it, "You save humans and animals alike."[51] Noah didn't just save animals; Noah was the savior of ecosystems. God's covenant was with all creation, "with all flesh that is on the earth."[52] That's why the eucharistic bread is shaped in a circle to symbolize the redemption of the whole cosmos.

In fact, part of Jesus's personal health-care regimen was mountain bathing, desert bathing, garden bathing, and water bathing—taking walks through the mountains, the desert, gardens, and shorelines where his spirit found the medicine it needed from these four natural landscapes. The world's greatest living poet, Wendell Berry, makes this as one of the striking features of the Last Adam, as much a gardener in his consciousness as the First Adam: "Jesus thought he was living in a holy world. . . . Much of the action and talk of the

Gospels takes place outdoors: on mountainsides, lakeshores, riverbanks, in fields and pastures, places populated not only by humans but by animals and plants. And these nonhuman creatures, sheep and lilies and birds, are always represented as worthy of, or as flourishing within, the love and care of God."[53]

But there is a serpent in every garden. God symbolized the curse of the fall by the serpent becoming a snake ("you will move on your belly and eat dust all the days of your life") and by the enmity between the serpent-snake and humanity ("he will crush your head, and you will strike his heel").[54] The Last Adam defeated the curse by crushing the serpent's head. At Golgatha, the place of the skull, the curse is broken and the skull is crushed. "Just as Moses lifted up the snake in the wilderness, so the Son of Man must be lifted up."[55] Jesus lifted up on a cross in a garden with a serpentine Golgatha is a fulfillment of the promise of Genesis 3:15.[56]

This story dating from the seventh century was a favorite of the bishop and theologian Isaac of Nineveh, the last saint to be recognized by all the East and the West apostolic branches of Christianity. Born in Qatar but bishop of northern Iraq, he was also known as Isaac the Assyrian. "An elder was once asked, 'What is a compassionate heart?' He replied, 'It is a heart on fire for the whole of creation, for humanity, for the birds, for the animals, for demons and all that exists. At the recollection and at the sight of them such a person's eyes overflow with tears owing to the vehemence of the compassion which grips his heart; as a result of his deep mercy his heart shrinks and cannot bear to hear or look on any injury or the slightest suffering of anything in creation.'"[57]

What would our lives be like if our days and nights were as immersed in nature as they are in technology?

—Richard Louv, "Reconnecting to Nature in the Age of Technology"

Our call to conserve is a call to see God in everything in life, and to see Christ's sovereignty in covenant living. In Hebrew theology, the covenant between God and humanity exists as sacred space. Within that relational space, or Shekinah, we know God, and find wholeness. It is that space God gives us that separates us as created from Creator, and yet binds us to God in relational union. In the image of our Creator, we need to find ways to create sacred space within our lives, our economies, the world, and our churches.

112

Conserving and Conceiving Sacred Space

Churches are focused on (1) getting people, (2) getting money, (3) getting things for free. Getting, getting, getting. When they should be giving, giving, giving. Most churches are more interested in self-support of their buildings and of their members than of supporting their communities. Our churches belong to God and are dedicated to God's mission in the world. Once a church becomes a territorial place instead of sacred space, it has ceased to be a conceiver community.

One parishioner said, "I'm tired of cleaning up after others who use our church." My reply: "Who are you 'preserving' it for?" We are called to conserve the covenant, not preserve the church. Our service can get tedious and tiring when not in the spirit of joy. Perhaps we need to ask how can we include more of our community in the making sacred of our sacred space, instead of milking the building as a "sacred cow" and bilking those who want to use it.

Even those who realize more than most that the "you" in "You are not alone" refers to all of creation have trouble escaping the need to control our own souls. Listen to the language of "preservation." We hear a lot about our need to "preserve" the earth.

I for one don't want anything to do with "preserving" the earth. You preserve pickles or pecks of pickled peppers. You preserve body parts. You preserve cadavers. You preserve little patches of wetlands that die a slow death because the dying life around them leeches their life right out of them. In sum, *preserve* is a control word that resists the continuing chaos of creation.

Nature should not be protected from humans by trying to exclude them. Rather, the saving of nature includes integrating humans and human needs into nature. Fewer walls, more space. More gardens, fewer houses. An economy of the garden is an economy of space, whether in the church or throughout the community.

A conserve-and-conceive economics thrives on creativity, entrepreneurial energy, interaction, relationships, and the faith to take risks. Sacred space is safe space, a space conserved to take risks that lead to abundant grace and incarnational faith. It is space for the power of Jesus to heal and bless. It is space for the Holy Spirit to move and change. It is space conserved for conceiving.

A community that is committed to making and conserving space in God's garden is also committed to a willingness to allow God to act. An economy of space is an economy of faith in the power of Jesus to create and renew. This is the one thing we haven't been willing to do. We want to "fix" things ourselves. We want to solve our own problems. We want to change things in ways we think will "Christianize" people, or bring them into our "boxes" and "house" them within our walls.

We do not trust the simple power of lifting up Christ. Jesus saves, and we do not. We proclaim Jesus. It is an economics of praise and a sacredness of space to grow and change.

Whereas a consumer economy deconstructs systems and divvies up creation, a conserver/conceiver economy takes creation whole and makes new possibilities for helping one another in ways that help the earth. God is not in the deconstruction business but in the redemption and construction business; not about creating dualisms but holism and holiness. When we join in God's creativity, we join the "family business" of birthing, healing, restoring, and conserving. Sacred space is birthing space. The Me/We of birthing is the Me/We of a conceiver economy. A Me/We whole gospel is not kingdom building but kingdom living.

And although the first birth is of the person, any pedagogy which stops at the Birthing of oneself is simply too narrow for our time. Birthing must spill over to the Birthing of just environments in society itself, for Birth and Breakthrough are "resurrections into justice."

—Maria Harris, *Dance of the Spirit*

Conserving and Conceiving the Commons

"The Commons" is space-making for a new kind of "good life" based on an economy of relationships, not an economy of "things." "The Commons" is not an economic "system" nor a specific place. It is an "economics" of wholeness, a new Me/We way of interacting with the world and one another that fosters full human flourishing and full integration as participants in "the good society."[58] The Commons is a space for birthing and cultivating relationships, where bonds are formed, friendships are forged, and creativity has space to flourish and bear fruit. Nobel laureate Elinor Ostrom, the first women to receive the Nobel Prize in economics (2009), is most famous for her argument that we need something beyond "common sense." We need "commons

114

sense," we need an ethic of the commons that is based on cooperation over competition, relationships over regulations.[59]

Common Ground for Common Good

The Commons[60] is where humans gather with other creatures on common ground for the common good. In commons-based thinking, helping oneself and helping others is intertwined with helping the earth. The fundamental question of our time is how you define the human and the common good. What is "human"? What is the "common"? What is the "good"? How thick a sense of the common good do we need for what is human? And how dependent is the human on the Commons?

The Commons is a composite term like *the state* and *the market* and the *Internet*.[61] In succinct form, *the Commons* means the wealth we share that we have received from God. But as the late Jonathan Rowe has shown,

> the commons includes our entire life support systems, both natural and social. The air and oceans, the web of species, wilderness and flowing water—all are parts of the commons. So are language and knowledge, sidewalks and public squares, the stories of childhood, the processes of democracy. Some parts of the commons are gifts of nature, others the product of human endeavor. Some are new, such as the internet, others are as ancient as soil and calligraphy. What they have in common is that they all "belong" to all of us, if that is the word. No one has exclusive rights to them.[62]

To conserve and conceive requires "commons" spaces and "commons thinking" in our churches and communities that are people based, not institution based; faith based, not society based; conception based, not consumption based. We need a garden-fresh economy with God's imprint on every new design. The Commons is an economy of receiving and giving, reciprocity and mutuality.

What was distinctive about the early church was not its economics. Early Christians did not practice what we know as "communism" or the abolition of private property or the absence of economic differentiation. What was unique about the economics of the early church was its spirit of the Commons. Capital was an exercise of trusteeship, less a right than a duty, to be put at the disposal of personal need and the dispersal of the common good. Property did not matter. Class distinctions did not matter. What mattered were the investments in social capital, not "what all owed to one" but "what one owed to all."

Living Fully, Living Well

For the early Christians, economics was not about how best to satisfy human desires but how best to desire what is fully human—the good, the true, the beautiful. For Jesus, the quality of life depended on the quality of relationships, not the quantity of resources. In fact, the word *wealth* originally meant "well-being" and "wellness"—both less dependent on higher wages than on higher relationships. God did not invent money. We did. Economic activity is not an end in itself. It is ordered to human life and welfare. Economics without teleology is pathology. When economics boasts the wrong benchmarks, the marks of the divine in the human get bleached. The end of our economic activity is human well-being, not wealth. Salvation, not sales.

Wealth should never be an end in itself. The guaranteeing of worldly power and success is not what Christianity is about. But if the gospel ever stops offering the poor a better life, you stop offering the gospel as good news.

A conserve-and-conceive economy is not just for the rich. It is also for the poor. Canadian scientist Ursula Franklin first came up with the designation "conserver society" in 1977 as a prescription for the future health of Canada. In a conserver society there is an ethics of enough where success is no longer excess, where rich and poor reconceive themselves in light of each other, and where humans "walk lightly" on the Commons.[63]

There is a growing disparity between a real human being and the facsimile of a real human being. Life with Christ is the ultimate human reality, the abundant life. Life without Christ is a life not fully lived. Jesus frees us from "the lie" to live "the Life." To conserve and conceive the Commons is to conserve and conceive the covenant. It is living life with Christ in the peace of God's pleasure. The Commons is not so much about the common good as about hearing God's voice say, "it is good."

The Commons is a wellness we share as Christians, as we conserve God in the midst of all relationships, all economies, all of life.

Dreaming the Commons

Picasso once said of Chagall: "I don't know where he gets those images. He must have an angel in his head."[64] Dreaming puts angels in the mind.

A conserve-and-conceive economy gives us permission to dream green dreams. To be green is to live in the presence of God, in the unconsuming fire of Christ's passion and power. To be green is to be aware of God's presence and creativity in all areas of life. In life you are usually moving in one of two directions: either toward heaven or away from hell—toward dreams of hope and nirvanas of advancement or away from never-agains. The current trend, unfortunately, seems to be in the direction of dreary "aways," not dreamy "towards."

After an "Oxbridge" summer, where I spent time teaching in both Oxford and Cambridge, I discovered that in British English, *dream* usually connotes a delusion, not a desire that can come true. There are various reasons for these depressants on dreams, but whatever the cause, to stop dreaming of a better world and a better Commons is to go dead. And humans get deadly when they go dead inside, when they shut themselves down from the future and stop living in the domain of dreams.

God designed us to dream, but these dreams are often screamed into silence by politics. Pilate's wife dreamed Jesus innocent. But the majority voices of a crowd won out over the minority voice of a dreamer. In a world of harsh political realities, dreams don't rate highly as default navigational directions.

The first thing to conserve is our dreams. Conserving the art of dreaming brings back the permission to conceive of the Commons.

The greatest achievement was at first and for a time a dream. The oak sleeps in the acorn; the bird waits in the egg; and in the highest vision of the soul a waking angel stirs. Dreams are the seedlings of realities.

—James Allen, *As a Man Thinketh*

Conserving for the Commons

To be in a holy relationship with God, each other, and the natural world is to treat creation as a subject, not an object. One cares for a subject; one uses an object. And when a subject one cares for is in peril, you step in and try to save it. *Saving* has two meanings. First is the traditional "waste not, want not" sense of conservation. Or as my Appalachian ancestors would put it, "Use it up; wear it out; make it do; or do without." Every home was a "Conservation Department," and every parent a conservation expert.

A conservation spirituality that saves the Commons in a practical sense would encourage its faithful to recycle, reduce carbon footprint, limit pesticide use, discourage food waste, empower indigenous and rural communities. It would foster a holy satisfaction with needs and not an unholy dissatisfaction with wants. Surveys of respondents show that mansionization spawns palatialization, as fewer and fewer people say they have all the things they need or are satisfied with their possessions.[65] In a conservation of the Commons, there is more of a saving up for something than paying off of something.

If people aren't filled, they will want. We live in a world that is seriously wanting. But the Commons for Christians begins with "The Lord is my shepherd, I shall not want." Conserving the Commons must start within the heart and flow outward to the hands and feet. If we are to change the way we conserve our world, we need to start with the way we conserve our faith. Conservation of the Commons always starts with our hearts and ends with our hands and feet. As Jesus said, "where your treasure is, there your heart will be also."[66]

Landfills don't compost or mulch or biodegrade. They mummify. They are our upside-down pyramids where future archeologists will find the symbols of a fallen civilization. Instead of a throwaway culture of planned obsolescence, here's a true conservation story, a story of how something can be cherished and cared for and actually appreciated over time.

In 1928, Allan Swift of West Hartford, Connecticut, bought a new Rolls Royce Phantom I. He drove the car for close to 77 years, and when he died at the age of 102 in October of 2005, he had the record for the longest ownership of a Rolls Royce. His "classic" is now worth a fortune.

But a new sense of saving—frugality, smaller homes, fewer possessions— defines economic activity (buying, selling, lending) within a larger realm of relationships where economic exchanges include a vast social life of friendship, patronage, gift swapping, and table life. In other words, we need to think of our circulation of goods and services less as economical and more as relational, much as people did in premodern, traditional societies. Here the Native American understanding of life can be especially instructive, and such things as the biodiversity initiatives of Native Circle of Food Program so important.

A relational sense of saving and conserving the Commons means a rediscovery of Sabbath in our lives and in our land. The soil needs to rest and be replenished. You can't let the soil (or a relationship) rest and heal by attempting to grow the same crop in it year after year. To be in love with the land is to change the crops with the changing soil, climate, and needs of the roots.

An economics that is based on planning rather than on cherished relationships is serving death, not life. Want to get God riled up? Think that nature is yours to do with what you will? Read the verses after Ezekiel 29:3 and see how God responds when God hears the arrogance of the human species say, "The Nile is mine; I made it for myself" (AT). The resurrection of Jesus was the fulfillment of creation, not the beat or defeat of creation. The earth itself is released from its bondage to sin and death.[67]

You must not worship things you have made yourself.
—Micah 5:13 (MNT)

A conserving of the Commons starts with a recognition of God's sovereignty and a response of humility.

A conservation of the Commons must also steer between the extremes of Mammonism, which worships things, and Manichaeism, where things are evil. The truth is people need "things" or "thingies," as I call them. As soon as God told Moses "You shall not make any graven image,"[68] Moses immediately ordered a brace of gilded cherubim over the mercy seat.[69] You and I are duvets of dirt, "thingies" if you will. The sacramental nature of material is built into the very creation of life. The key is not to idolize matter nor to demonize it. In fact, in some ways, we need a less carefree, more caring relationship with (materiality) objects and artifacts. A consuming culture is a synthetic, discarding culture. A conserving culture is an organic, saving culture that cares for things and thus needs fewer of them.

Besides, the problem is not with things but with us. Nathaniel Hawthorne wrote a strange tale called "Earth's Holocaust." In the story, the Earth's inhabitants, "overburdened with an accumulation of worn-out trumpery, determined to rid themselves of it by a general bonfire." All night long a stranger with a cynical smile stood in the background, watching them bring all the things that they had built to mess up their lives: war implements, liquor, tobacco. Whatever was brought was thrown into a bigger and bigger bonfire.

Finally the stranger approached the people doing the burning and said: "There is one thing that these wiseacres have forgotten to throw into the fire, and without which all the rest of the conflagration is just nothing at all; yes, though they have burned the earth itself to a cinder."

"And what may that be?" someone asked.

The stranger replied, "What but the human heart itself . . . And, unless they hit upon some method of purifying that foul cavern, forth from it will reissue all the shapes of wrong and misery—the same old shapes or worse ones— which they have taken such a vast deal of trouble to consume to ashes. . . . O, take my word for it, it will be the old world yet!"[70]

To change the heart is to write God's ID upon it. To change the heart is to return to the relational economy of the Commons.

Conceiving the Commons

Conceiving the Commons involves more than just imagining a new way to shop, a new social order, or a new economic system. It involves conceiving of a sense of boundaries, conceiving spaces for creativity, repenting of wrong-doing, learning new relational ways to live creatively and constructively, trusting, and finding pleasure in the world and in each other. It acknowledges the Jesus doctrine that the good life of an individual is always realized in community with others.

A cowboy was prosecuted for stealing another man's outhouse. "What's so special about the outhouse?" someone asked. A neighbor answered, "Wasn't his outhouse."

Living in abundance, each under our own fig tree, requires personal responsibility and communal accountability. The Commons is a Me/We venture.

A sense of the precariousness and preciousness of life, a sense of limits and limitations, is what links our actions to the great chain of being called the Commons. It's also what charges a single purchase with significance for the Commons. Without a sense of restraints and restrictions, we are alienated from, not connected to, our context and environment. Every decision we make affects our relationships and must be approached with responsibility and humility. With every move we make, the "body" reverberates.

Jacques Derrida's straight-faced claim that to feed his own cat is to neglect all the other cats in the world, and thus to garner guilt, is not a bogus bonus for guilt in a world with a surfeit of reasons. It is a reflection of the reality that our every decision, including feeding the cat, makes us complicit in the health or sickness of the entire universe.

However, in a relational world, the Me exerts the greatest impact on the We not with more regulations but with more freedom to exercise personal responsibility and the classical virtues of moderation, prudence, courage, and justice. The logic of the Commons that guides both individual and community behavior are summarized by Rosabeth Moss Kanter for the corporate community as follows:

1. **common purpose** (seeing every entity and decision as social, not just among shareholders but stakeholders too);

2. **longer-term view** (the tyranny of short-termism is one of the key flaws in the current model of market capitalism, which desperately needs an ethos of short-term sacrifices and deferred gratification for wider gains);

3. **emotional engagement** (transmit an ethos that enables self-regulation and peer-regulation).

To be human is to be hedged by limitations. Humans were not meant so much to put away the limits as to push against the limits. Life in the Commons has to have boundaries. Like playing tennis without a net, you can't get better at life without boundaries. Liberty needs limits to exist.

Even love has limits. There was a loving elephant who noticed an ostrich leave her eggs to get a drink of water. The elephant ambled over to the nest, and, out of pure love, sat on the ostrich eggs to keep them warm. Love can be an elephantine thing if we're not careful.

If I were to wish for anything, I should not wish for wealth and power, but for the passion of the potential, that eye which everywhere, ever young, ever burning, sees possibility. Pleasure disappoints, not possibility.

—Søren Kierkegaard, "Diapsalmata"

But it also must have open spaces, commons spaces, in which to dream, create, live, conceive. To conceive the Commons is to love the Sabbath, enjoy the natural world, raise the roof, and let the imagination soar.

Finding joy in the natural world and its sensory pleasures is not pagan but pious play.

Why is modern Western childhood much less rich and happy than those in the past or elsewhere? One reason is that today's children are more enclosed and removed from nature than in times past or in some other cultures. Eighty percent of young children's dreams are about animals. If nature is essential for the formation of a healthy child's psyche, with trees essential to childhood dreams of "questing" more than either the sea or the mountains,[71] then our children are in peril. Childhood has become increasingly sanitized, commoditized, and monetized, lacking in the space and terrain for children to discover their human nature.

Gardeners who conserve and conceive their gardens know how to do both letting go and letting be. They know how to conceive of new gardens and places, how to seed, spread, and to innovate, as well as how to cultivate and conserve the soil. The Commons resides in a tension between conserving boundaries and conceiving open spaces.

Conceiving the Commons is also a high-risk endeavor that involves "resistance" living. As Christians, it requires us to live daringly different within an old-world environment. It challenges us to create new environments in the midst of or on the outskirts of stale systems and institutions. It is "get off the grid" living with high-stakes faith. It means living a garden life as the "help" and not the "master."

An old story about a monk from the ancient world has him saying that a person must live in peace with all other persons, including his enemies, but *not* with the enemies of God.[72]

Conserving and conceiving the Commons involves a counterstory of resistance living, as the forces of destruction are beaten back daily. Resistance living means more than getting off the grid or growing/producing your own food. Resistance living means each person assumes the role of editor rather than passive consumer, with a sturdily resistant strain of push-back running through every attempt to enclose or gate the Commons. In the words of the fourth-century bishop Ambrose, "Not merely the possessions of the earth, but the very sky, air, and sea are claimed for the use of the rich few. . . . The earth belongs to all, not to the rich."[73]

Michel de Certeau, in his famous work *The Practice of Everyday Life*, spoke of "resistance" as the daily deflections of power by the damaging systems of consumption from which we can't escape. These resistance tactics can take many forms of actions: murmurings, ruses, simulations, joyful celebrations, walkings, and many more seizings of the "spaces within which to maneuver."

Hope of all the ends of the earth / and of the farthest seas.
— Psalm 65:5 NRSV

Some things don't change. St. John Chrysostom said that "not to enable the poor to share in our goods is to steal from them," for "the goods we possess are not ours, but theirs."[74] They had the same problem back then that we do today. Only the scale has changed. But that change in scale makes all the difference in the world.

Why can't the church get ahead on the creation front? Why is it that poor suffering people move us but the suffering of the planet and poor Earth leaves us cold? In many cases, from Bangladesh to Burma, it's the suffering of the planet that increases the suffering of the poor. Conceiving the Commons means repentance from old systems and ushering in the new. At the same time, conception shifts the focus from the repentance of collateral damage to the rejoicing of collateral good, collateral truth, and collateral beauty.[75]

The activity of the human spirit is often an atrocity of the human spirit. In fact, there is something of the killer in us that requires repentance. The RAF bombed Berlin nineteen times between August 1943 and March 1944, killing nearly ten thousand civilians, three thousand airmen, and untold plant and animal species, not to mention art and architecture. The strafe bombings and "collateral damage" of killings of the innocent at Dresden[76] stand alongside the atomic bombings of Hiroshima and Nagasaki as moral question marks stamped forever on the forehead of the human species.

In the epilogue of their 1992 book, *Easter Island, Earth Island*, the archaeologists Paul Bahn and John Flenley are explicit about the environmental impact of human beings. The Easter islanders, they write, "carried out for us the experiment of permitting unrestricted population growth, profligate use of resources, destruction of the environment, and boundless confidence in their religion to take care of the future. The result was an ecological disaster leading to a population crash. . . . Do we have to repeat the experiment on a grand scale? Is the human personality always the same as that of the person who felled the last tree?"[77]

The last tree. The last passenger pigeon. The last Dodo bird. The last Tasmanian tiger. Soon the last polar bear? The last tuna? The last gorilla? Even after we knew whales were barely hanging on to life, more than three million were killed during the twentieth century by Norway, Japan, the USSR, and the UK alone. We seem to kill the very things that care for us the most and kiss us the best. If police were doing an objective "profile" of our species, would we be classified as "serial killers beyond reason"?[78]

The egoism at the heart of consumerism is what is destroying the environment, and thickening the "blanket" that is wrapping planet Earth in its heat, raising the waters, and defiling the air.

A conceiver Commons must go from ego to eco: from systems that feed our egos to a Commons that is an ecology of Me/We love and grace.

An indicative must go with an imperative. The important thing is to begin our conserving and conceiving somewhere, to take daily actions to slow the inertia of destructive consumption and safeguard the forces of conservation and reclamation. Our actions, even of a minimal nature, can have great cumulative impact. When we refuse to buy certain goods made in a certain way or based on exploitation of the poor, we build bridges on the Commons between ourselves and the rest of humanity. When we put our money where our mouth is, we begin to make, in Shelley's words, "the pains and pleasures of [the] species' become our own."[79]

Buy This, Birth That: A Model for Conceiving the Commons

A Me/We gospel stands against a culture of consumption and instead grows a cultured garden of conception. A conserve and conceive culture creates boundaries where we can say yes to certain forms of consumption and no to others, according to the conceiver principle of "buy this, birth that."

In a consumption culture, when we buy this, we bury that. In a conception culture, when we buy something, that selection allows us to creatively birth something new in the world, something that adds to God's creativity and mission in some extraordinary new way. Everything we buy should birth something, especially beauty, goodness, or truth. In fact, the Commons only survives by conceiving new ways of imagining and expressing itself.

It is better to conceive than consume. Even though Jesus said "I came eating and drinking,"[80] unlike the simple-living John, "the kingdom of God is not mere eating and drinking (consuming) but righteousness and peace and joy"[81] (conceiving), conceiving the fruit of the Spirit. Churches of the Commons are conception centers, and our sanctuaries "birthing rooms" for the Spirit.

Apart from Me, you can do nothing.
The Person abiding in Christ bears some fruit,
and can bear more fruit, and much fruit.

—John 15:5-8 AT

Conceiving is turning water into wine, rocks into living stones, death into life, tax collectors into reapers of souls. The world changes through disciples of Jesus who conserve and conceive the Truth of the Spirit.

The biblical alternative to an "I consume therefore I am" world is an "I conceive therefore we are" society.

- A consumer culture is where people find their identity in what they purchase. A conceiver culture is where people find their identity in whom they love—God and neighbor. God in the midst of relationships is a We identity for every Me.

- A consumer life is something you grasp. A conceiver life is something you grow when God grows in you.

- A consumer culture exhibits a me-first consciousness. A conceiver culture exhibits a God is sovereign consciousness of humility and service.

- A consumer culture consumes for its own sake, straining the social fabric. A conceiver culture consumes for the good of the individual in personal responsibility for the whole.

- A consumer culture focuses on short-term objects/projects. A conceiver culture focuses on the long-term and sustainable relationships.

- A consumer culture assesses success in terms of what contributes to higher productivity and higher consumption. A conceiver culture assesses wellness in terms of the deeper and more lasting purposes of life in Christ.

- A consumer culture loves lists of things for sale. A conceiver culture loves lists of things for free, for exchange, for barter, for life dollars, as well as for sale, and treasures relationships above materiality.

- A consumer culture is for takers where the "pursuit of happiness" is paramount. A conceiver culture is for givers where the "pursuit of meaning" and identity in Christ is primary.[82]

- In a consumer culture the "good life" all depends on an individual context—the quality of one's own experiences. In a conceiver culture the "good life" all depends on God's graces and a free salvation—the quality of the human experience in relationship.[83]

- In a consumer culture, the economy becomes a "machine." In a conceiver culture, the economy becomes a "beating heart."[84] In a consumer culture the market is master. In a conceiver culture the market is servant.[85]

- A consumer culture tickles the fancy. A conceiver culture triggers the imagination. The Bible contains more good stories than any other book its size. But these are conception stories, not consumption stories—with plotlines that highlight a conceiver not a consumer consciousness.

- A consumer culture passively consumes an already prefabricated culture. A conceiver culture throws off the chains of passivity and creates a God-blessed creative culture, creating rich, deep layers of artisanal life, as fertile and rich in God's presence as soil.

- In a consumer culture, you live your choices and you become the sum of your choices. In a conceiver culture, you live your chosenness and you become the sum of your summons, as the Holy Spirit serves summons on each of us to serve.

- In a consumer culture, novelty is the currency; in a conceiver culture, innovation is the currency.

- A consumer culture travels down Madison Avenue and Rodeo Drive. A conceiver culture travels down the Jericho Road and the King's Highway.

- A consumer culture is governed by the will to kill. A conceiver culture is governed by the will to fill—to "fill the earth"[86] and fill the hungry with good things.[87]

- A consumer world identifies more freedom with more choices.[88] A conceiver world identifies more freedom with more necessities, the most important of which is becoming free and joyful in God because that is who you are. It is for freedom, not for free markets, that Christ has set us free. What is freedom for? To consume? Or to conserve and conceive? Jesus's deepest freedom was that he could do no other than the Father's will—he is compelled to go to Jerusalem to suffer and die.[89] Supreme freedom is to do what makes who you are, not to be all you wish to be.

A buy-this, birth-that mentality does two things: conserves and conceives. True originality is faithful to the "originals" and especially the originating creation story. A love of conformity is complementary to, not contradictory of, a love of originality. We don't honor the future by dishonoring the past. True originality is not a mere recycling of the original but a fresh imagining, a reconceiving of its origins.

Conceiving a Me/We Economy

What does bearing "fruit" look like? What makes it fruit of the Spirit and not just secular "good-ness" such as the Fair Trade Movement? Is Christianity "implied" in any act of goodness? Or is there something more transformational that happens when we let Christ move and work within people in a Me/We way?

Creative entrepreneurship may bolster creativity, collaboration, entrepreneurial spirit. But what happens when Jesus followers and the Church become artisanal, creative, collaborative? What happens when faith becomes proclamation and praise, and fruit becomes changed lives and changed ideas of what "eco-nomy" truly can be? A conceiver economy is about change and renewal. And as my mother used to say, "Little is big when God is in it."

God's first fiat? *Let there be light.* Every time we conceive, we bring light to life, and thereby are re-creating that first fiat: "Let there be light."

The Lucifer cry of "Consume" is the voice of the anti-Christ. The Jesus cry of "Conceive" is the voice of the crucified Christ. The difference between a life of consumption versus a life of conception is the difference between the Market God's "Good Life" vs. The Maker God's "Abundant Life."

A consumer culture is based on the mantra, "I consume, therefore I am independent." A conceiver culture is based on the mantra, "I conceive, therefore we are part of God's garden world." A consumer culture collects the oyster shells and discards (sells/hoards) the pearls. A conceiver culture grows authentic pearls, especially the pearl of great price. A church that finds joy in receiving from God is a church that gives; and a giving church is a church that "runs over." A church that finds joy in consuming is a church that conceals; and a concealing church is a church that "draws back" from the truth. Both *eros* love and *agapē* love are reproductive/conceptive, but where erotic love conceives for the Me, agapic love conceives for the We by giving itself away (unless a grain of wheat falls).

God conceived of me; my parents conceived me. And there are lots of concepts, like "concept cars," that have been conceived of but never conceived. There is a grave confusion between "conceiving of" and "conceiving." There can be lots of "conceiving of" with very little "conceiving." A consumption culture needs to be challenged and deflected by a conception culture—a people who consume challenged by a people who conceive.

And Adam knew [yada] Eve his wife; and she conceived.
—Genesis 4:1 KJV

Fruit bearing (conceiving) involves "knowing." The Hebrew word for "know" is *yada*, a deeply relational word suggesting the highest in intimacy, as when a husband and wife "know" each other sexually. Knowing in a relational context results in conceiving.[90]

- When God "knew" (*yada*) God, the Triune God conceived, and the universe was born.

128

- When God "knew" (*yada*) the universe, they conceived: and Adam was born.

- When body "knew" (*yada*) spirit, they conceived, and a soul was born.

- When Adam "knew" (*yada*) Eve, they conceived, and Cain and Abel were born.

- When height "knew" (*yada*) depth, they conceived, and three-dimensionality was born.

- When transcendence "knew" (*yada*) immanence, they conceived, and a Cruciform Christ was born.

- When the disciples "knew" (*yada*) the Holy Spirit, when blood knew breath, they conceived, and the church was born.

- When seed "knows" soil, a plant is conceived, and a flower is born.

- When sun "knows" cloud, they conceive, and a rainbow is born.

All true "knowing" leads to conception. Most especially, when we "know" God, we conceive, and our conceptions are participations with God in the ongoing creation of a Garden City, a "new heaven and a new earth." Conception is the mother of all invention.

The question of life is not what are you consuming but what are you conceiving? For Christians, the ultimate "conceiving" is for Christ to be born in us. In the fourteenth century, Meister Eckhart claimed that all disciples become Virgin Marys, or as he put it "mothers of Christ," conceivers of Christ for the world. "God is waiting eternally to be born in each of us," he said.[91] A millennium before Eckhart, the fourth-century archbishop of Milan, Saint Ambrose, put it like this: "If according to the flesh, one woman is the mother of Christ, according to the truth, Christ is the fruit of us all."[92]

My little children, for whom I am again suffering birth pangs until Christ is completely and permanently formed (molded) within you.[93]

—Galatians 4:19 AMP

All the primal energy of the universe, the force that Edith Sitwell refers to as "The wasteful Gardener Who to grow one flower / Your life, like a long-petalled Sun—has strewn the infinite"[94] now becomes the God unborn, living and breathing inside the womb of a woman, living and breathing outside the womb of the earth, that we might be partners in the redemption of the world.

Replace the words *believe in* in the Apostle's Creed with the words *do/with*. In other words, "I do acts of mercy along with God," and "I do acts of healing along with Jesus," and "I do creative work with the power of the Holy Spirit" and "I do forgiveness of sins with the power of Jesus." What we "do" is art, and as people created in the Creator's image, we are expected to "do" our faith "with" God, to take God's story, with all its plot and power, and paint it along with who we are—with our specialness and specificity. This is the on-going incarnation. God is the Great artist. We are God's junior apprentices. When we allow ourselves to be guided, molded, inbreathed, empowered by the Holy Spirit, we can't help but conceive what is good, true, and beautiful.

When Christ is born in you, you will conceive the fruit of the Spirit. When you see amazing things happen in the world, you know that God is somewhere in it. How do you know that Christ is born in you? You know that:

- Christ is born in you . . . when you conceive food at a soup kitchen for the homeless.

- Christ is born in you . . . when you conceive mentoring for a student who loves learning because of your influence.

- Christ is born in you . . . when you conceive a Little League team that takes shape from your coaching.

- Christ is born in you . . . when you conceive hospitality for a stranger in your home or on the road.

- Christ is born in you . . . when you conceive compliments to your friends when they've done nothing special but be your friend.

- Christ is born in you . . . when you conceive a smile by saying thank you at the slightest provocation.

- Christ is born again . . . when you conceive the knowledge that, with God, all things are conceivable.

- Christ is born again . . . when you "conceive hopes greater than your fears" (John Newton).[95]

We take for granted how radically participatory this concept of "conception" is at our peril. God's basic design concept seems to be complex, emerging, self-organizing, adaptive. God created unfinished forms of life that were charged with "going on to perfection"—forms of life capable of further development.

Conceiving a Christ Economy

Jesus said that things might most reliably be known for what they were by examining their fruits. We are called to be "fruitful," not just "faithful." What does it look like to be faithful and fruitful?

The most essential component of a conceiver's credentials is a crazed passion for beauty, truth, and goodness. What is the joy of your desiring? What are the desires of your heart? Lucifer light makes consumption the joy of our desiring . . . and desiring itself the sheer joy of desiring. Jesus Light makes mercy, new creation, the coming kingdom the joy of our desiring, especially "Jesu, Joy of Man's Desiring."

Like all of us, I have a few biblical texts I return to over and over, that seem to speak something very, very deeply to me. Here's one: "Beware of false prophets, who come to you in sheep's clothing but inwardly are ravenous wolves. You will know them by their fruits."[96]

The true and false prophets look the same. We can't tell them apart by the "truths" they utter. Our telling "the truth" is little evidence that we ourselves are helpful or godly. The only way to tell what's what is by the "fruits."

I have been learning the hard way that there are lots of truths I can speak that are not fruitful. They don't assist anyone, and do not further God's kingdom. Sometimes, I need to keep a lid on the truths I know in order to truly love someone.

Fruit bearing, however, is not just displaying the characteristics of a Christian life. It is also passing on the covenant of your Christ-identity to others and to future generations. We both "bear" the mark (incarnation) of Jesus and "bear" (conceive) the fruit that is Jesus to the world. A true conceiver community is simultaneously exampling and sampling the fruits of the gospel to the world.

Conceiving as Imaging Jesus (Me)

A conceiver society is measured by three conceivings or "fruits":

1. Beauty

2. Truth

3. Goodness

The "Three Transcendentals," or the "three transcendentals of being," stand as some of the highest achievements born of the dance of medieval Christian scholasticism and Greek philosophy.[97] A conceiver life introduces into the mess and middle of everyday life beauty, truth, and goodness. This is what it means to live a "fruitful" or "meaningful" life, one that is lived with a trajectory toward these three transcendentals.

But if beauty, truth, goodness are attributes of God, then Jesus added love as the issuer of all of the other three. In fact, when the Apostle Paul speaks of bearing the incarnational marks of being a Jesus follower in the first-century churches, he begins with love as "the greatest of these." The "fruits of the Spirit" in all their manifestations come from loving God.

"I am the true vine, and my Father is the husbandman.
Every branch in me that bears not fruit he takes away; and every
branch that bears fruit, he purges, that is may bring forth more fruit."

—John 15:1-2

Love gestates creativity. God's act of creating was an act of love. The Tree of Life (Jesus) is the restoration of the relational unity that bears the fruits of God's creation. The only tree we must not touch is the one tree that separates Me from We—the one that creates dichotomies, separations, and divisions.

Forbidden Fruit Creates Many Jams

—church sign

Consumer society creates a "selfie" world, where every person goes all out for Me. Consumerism is naturally divisional. And a divisional society becomes obsessed with justice. Not the justice of the Bible, however, which is primarily directed toward ourselves and our own behavior. Not God's justice, which is cloaked and soaked in mercy. A "selfie" world covets being the "judges" of everyone else.

In the scriptures the Hebrew word for *judge* means "savior" or "redeemer." The book of Judges is better named "the book of Saviors." We are not in the justice business, and justice is not the end of a life of faith. Justice is God's business, and the byproduct of holiness. The end of discipleship is not a life of justice. The end of discipleship is a life of holiness, of which is one expression of a holy life. God's justice can only be defined in terms of love, mercy, truth, beauty, and goodness. These are the fruits that grow in the trees of the Commons. These are the fruits of the Tree of Life, not the Tree of Division. And a fruit-bearing economy is an economy in which the Me serves the We. They are inseparably bonded. Jesus is the true Commons.

"Every good tree bears good fruit, but a bad tree bears bad fruit."

—Matthew 7:17 NKJV

How do you know you are growing in the image of God? How do you know if your church is maturing spiritually?

Here's how. You answer these questions:

Are you conceiving?

Are you "being fruitful?"

Are the "fruits of the Spirit" being conceived in your life and in the life of the Commons?

When Paul talks about the fruit of the Spirit in his writings,[98] it is always referred to as singular. It is not the fruits of the spirit but the fruit of the Spirit. The fruit may have multiple manifestations or attributes ("love, joy, peace, patience, kindness, generosity, faithfulness, gentleness, and self-control"[99]), but it is singular, because it comes from one seed, the seed of the Last Adam. If anyone produces fruit that is not of Christ, it is not the Living Story of the Torah but, in fact, a counterfeit story.

We worship God because it is true and good and beautiful to do so, not because we get something out of it. God is to be loved and enjoyed, not employed.[100] To use God for any other end, whether the ends be economic or political or whatever, is to take God's name in vain. The old social gospel too easily elides the spiritual and the political.

When you and I stand at the bar of Judgment Day, we are not going to be asked: How big was your membership? How strong was your budget? But we will be asked: Did you love people? Did you lift up Christ? Did you introduce people to the Savior? How faithful were your relationships? Let me taste your fruit. The fruit of a tree is that tree come to consciousness. The fruit of a life is that life come to consciousness.

The people who hate Darwin the most practice social Darwinism the best. But notice that Jesus doesn't say that the tree needed to produce. Jesus always talks bearing fruit. And there is a difference.

To borrow from the Gospel of John, Jesus said, "Those who remain in me, with me in them, bear fruit in plenty."[101] Productivity has to do with giving and giving and giving until you end up with some product outside of yourself to which you can look and say, "I made that." Bearing fruit has to do with receiving and receiving and receiving until the fruit of the spirit begins to ripen inside of you. God then looks at it and says, "I made that!"

You will know them by their fruits. Are grapes gathered from thorns, or figs from thistles?

—Matthew 7:16 NRSV

We are the fruit. Take an apple. It has a pit, a pit-filled, pitiful core. It has hard, sometimes grizzly skin. It has soft pulp that turns brown when exposed and unprotected from the air. When it ripens too much, it decays quickly. But that is the nature of fruit. And it is nourishing. Fruit is meant to be eaten from the vine, to be conceived, consumed, and reconceived. When we bear the fruit, we must not let it rot on the vine, but it must be given away. The kind of fruit you bear will be revealed in the nourishing power it has for others.

God calls us to live lives of fruitfulness. Jesus uses the analogy of the vine and the branches. He is the Vine. We are the branches. We are more than "channels" of Christ. We are "branches" of the Vine, which is Christ. South African missiologist David Bosch explains the difference: "A channel remains unaffected by what flows through it, but a branch has, first of all, to absorb the nutritive power which comes to it from the roots and trunk. It has to make all this a part of itself, and allow itself to be affected, and renewed and transformed by that power. Only after having assimilated such energy can the branch impart it to the fruit."[102]

If the branches abide in the Vine, letting the joy and juice of Christ not merely flow through them but become part of them, then fruit will grow. Because of that absorption of energy, God can even make branches bear fruit out of season. One of Jesus's most disturbing moments is his cursing of the fig tree that would not bear fruit "out of season" to feed a hungry Messiah.

For one who understands and observes that this world and its goods are for uses intended by God, no quantity of goods is too great; for all others, any quantity is too great.[103]

—St. Augustine

Jesus is not just the smartest person who ever lived. Jesus is also the most creative person who ever lived. When nurtured at the Vine, the church could be a wellspring of creativity. But Christianity is like great art. For there to be truly original art, there must be submission to basic disciplines, mastery of the scriptures, a passion for an imagined creation, and a willingness to submit to the Creator.

Blessed is the man that trusteth in the LORD, and whose hope the LORD is.
For he shall be as a tree planted by the waters, and that spreadeth out her roots
by the river, and shall not see when heat cometh, but her leaf shall be green; and
shall not be careful in the year of drought, neither shall cease from yielding fruit.

—Jeremiah 17:7-8 KJV

In the Commons of a Me/We economy, the question must be "What are you conceiving?" *not* "What did you buy that for?" Are you conceiving beauty, truth, and goodness? Faith, hope, and love? We are imagers of God. The church as the Commons is an imagined faith community. Only in each of our imaginings lies the full breadth and depth of our communion. What shapes and structures our broader imaginings is the image of Jesus.

If Christ is the Light of We, you might think of Me as his Great Menorah. Through the lighting of our menorah, we conceive Christ within the world through his light. If the seven candles of the menorah stand for seven *I*s that remind us how to continually conceive Christ in, through and among us, then these are the *I*s I would choose:

Incarnation/Identity
Intuition   Innovativeness
Intentionality   Initiative
Integrity   Intimacy

The seven-branched candle-stand called *the menorah* stood in front of the holiest place in the temple as the Hebrew symbol of the covenant relationship between Yahweh and the people. The menorah is made up of seven candles for the seven days of creation. These candles light the "way" of the Shema. The center candle is the light of God, the light of the Sabbath. The menorah was both the Tree of Life from the garden and the lamp of Moses symbolizing the presence of the divine in the burning bush. The menorah was never allowed to go out.

The Letter to the Hebrews shows how the layout and furnishings of the temple were used by the Holy Spirit to prefigure and sort out the role of

Christ. Hence the menorah is still used in various strands of Eastern Ortho-doxy. It stands on the altar to represent the light of Christ and the fire of the Spirit that orients our way, illuminates our path, infuses us with the luster and light of the divine. According to Jerome (237–420), the lampstand is the law, the light is Christ, and the seven candle tips are the graces of the Holy Spirit—each tip a tip-off to incarnation.

Each of the seven candles can be seen as means of (en)lightenment and discernment of Jesus in the world. Each tip flickers constant reminders of the impartation of Christ in us and his "inspiritment" into our lives. Each metaphor of inspiritment helps us embody and enlighten our faith with a Christ identity.

Conservers and conceivers are the acolytes of this Great Menorah. John Wesley called such reminders "means of grace." The "inspiriting" process of re-minding and re-membering he called "sanctification" or "holiness." *Holiness* is the name given to the phenomenon of falling deeper and deeper in love with Jesus. Sanctification is the maturation of love, the lifelong lighting of the tips of the menorah. To move the metaphor from menorah to marble, sancti-fication deepens the sheen of the divine in each one of us, as the sculpting of the Spirit brings out the Jesus lineaments of the marble.

Tip 1: Incarnation/Identity

The center candle, representing the incarnate presence of God, is the cen-terpiece of truth-telling. To "tell" the truth is not so much a practice of debat-ing as a practice of discerning and demonstrating Truth. The center candle of the menorah is the *I* of identity, the most important of our tips that allows us to keep aligned to the Truth in everyday life.

There is only one "Jesus" or "Big J." But we are all summoned to be "little j's." In a world that fashions identity out of possessions, lifestyles, achieve-ments, styles, the identity of Jesus disciples is formed from the stories, meta-phors, rituals, and relics of the Christian tradition. Every biblical story has the whole story nestled within it, and if we live the Jesus story, our story will too. That makes the incarnation ongoing, as we become a third testament or fifth gospel.

If only disciples of Jesus were as incarnational as viruses, who continually adapt and combine to thrive in new environments.

The Black Death in medieval Europe ended in the winter of 1351–1352.

Caused by the bubonic plague (as well as anthrax), it was the worst epidemic in recorded history. It killed 25 to 45 percent of the populations where it struck in only four years. Venice, the only Italian city to keep accurate death records, reveals that the Black Death killed 60 percent of its population. Yet as bad as this was, Nathan Wolf contends that "Some of the greatest killers of humankind have been viruses: smallpox, measles, influenza and HIV. To a much greater extent than bacteria (plague, syphilis, tuberculosis, cholera), viruses are slippery customers, shape-shifters that cheerfully evolve and combine to emerge in new incarnations."[104] Their success as the greatest killers of humankind (smallpox, measles, influenza, HIV) are trophies to the power of new incarnations.

Once we personate (*not* impersonate) Christ's identity within us, we can use other "tips" to keep us on the path of Truth. These tips are integrity, initiative, intentionality, intuition, innovativeness, and intimacy.

When someone retires, I want to write them a note:
"Glad you have found a harbor. We shall miss you on the high seas."

—Leonard Sweet

Tip 2: Integrity

Integrity is the refusal to paint things over. It is the resolve to be a strong ally of truth, even when it's uncomfortable and messy. We love to quote Martin Luther's admonition to "sin boldly," but forget the whole context which is all about living out of integrity and not some bogus boilerplate: "If you are a preacher of grace, then preach a true and not a fictitious grace; if grace is true, you must bear a true and not a fictitious sin. God does not save people who are only fictitious sinners. Be a sinner and sin boldly, but believe and rejoice in Christ even more boldly, for he is victorious over sin, death, and the world."[105]

Of course, in every age human decency, not to mention trust, has been in short supply. To prove paternity in Elizabethan times, for example, a woman would be questioned as to the identity of the baby's father during childbirth when the pain and emotion were seen as guarantors of truthfulness. Integrity is all about the authenticity of relationships and experiences in the big moments and in the small. The very word *occasional*, as people like Goethe used the word, meant responding to a particular moment or occasion with bull-bodied integrity of being and authenticity of emotions without being flippant or casual.

Tip 3: Initiative

God always takes the initiative with us, whether we are behaving well or badly. "I will seduce her," Yahweh says through the prophet Hosea, speaking of Israel as his bride.[106] St. Ambrose called the church at its best a *casta meretrix* or a "chaste harlot" that God is always pursuing and purifying, a metaphor first used by Hosea for God's chosen people.

When God created humankind, God granted humans the gift of free will, allowing us to participate or not in the divine nature. This choice for God or against God, for participation or for passivity, is the most fundamental decision in human life. A covenant is a two-way promise that requires the initiative of participation rather than passivity on our part. Passivity is the moral equivalent of kudzu—once it takes hold, it takes over everything and inaction triumphs. The opposite of initiative is sloth and solitaire.

You might call initiative putting shoes on faith. Shoes prepare us to journey across all terrains and to go wherever we are led no matter how treacherous or unpaved. They help us run, dance, leap, gain traction, conceive of great and amazing things. They allow us to go the extra mile as we make tracks for those "three transcendentals" in the world. But shoes won't prevent your feet from getting dirty or tired from the road. Rather, initiative gives the means to stay grounded in the truth in the fight against inertia and the status quo.

Former Wyoming senator Alan K. Simpson used the phrase "Who gave you your Jesus shoes?" when someone was being too judgmental and nosy. Jesus shoes don't run over people, or run down people, but run toward people in service and love and put on others' shoes in empathy and compassion.

Don't let making a living prevent you from making a life.
—John R. Wooden, *Wooden*

All true reverence has some reticence. Faith is trusting but truthful: "Lord, I believe; help my unbelief!"[107] The play of piety and doubt is sometimes called "negative capability," the ability to transcend one's own context and to live in a place of ambiguity without the need for nailing everything down. Poet John Keats (1795–1821) coined the term to explain a receptivity to life free from the need to always categorize or define the unfamiliar. The initiative of negative capability involves a resistance to rigid conformity, to well-paved roads, to preconceived thought structures. If Jesus's first disciples had a hard time walking in his shoes, we shouldn't be surprised at the challenges. But when we don the shoes of initiative, we walk in the world in brand new ways but with surefooted gait as we follow the Way.

Tip 4: Intentionality

Intentionality is that focus that feeds us and fixes us firmly in the Lord of All in the face of inertia's pull of the everyday. Intentionality is the reminder that we need to be nourished each and every day in the experience of God that we need to encounter Jesus fresh every morning and renew our covenant with him daily. Intentionality is making provision for the journey to the point where discipleship is provision without baggage. Intentionality is what keeps us playing and walking in God's garden instead of in devil's field. Intentionality is what keeps it from being easier to listen to a new idea defensively and say "Why?" than to listen to a new idea receptively and say "Why not?"

The intentionality of daily baked bread is a form of "holy communion" with Christ that keeps us awake to the Truth, aware of the Way, and stewards of the mysteries of the leaven that can feed generations of disciples for the Life. A conceiver society distinguishes freshly baked bread from mere manna, and plants the seed of Christ for future followers.

The gospels were not written merely to document the stories and sayings of a dead person but to convey what Jesus is doing and speaking today—a totally unique literary genre. Whether the intentionality of prayer, which keeps our faith on track, or the intentionality of a lifelong vocation of devotion, intentionality is what makes everything we say and do, everything we sing and write, but a fragment of one great confession: "Jesus is Lord."

Tip 5: Intuition

Richard Pipes was a Professor of Russian History at Harvard. He became a member of Ronald Reagan's National Security team. This is his journal entry reporting on the first NSC meeting he attended in October 1981: "RR totally lost, out of his depth, uncomfortable. After making some common-sensical remarks did not speak for forty-five minutes or so; when he finally spoke it was to sigh, 'Oh, boy!'—meaning 'what am I to make of this mess?'"

But Pipes goes on to say that Reagan "understood remarkably well—intuitively rather than intellectually—the big issues."[108]

Most of us are trained more in Moneyball (look at the data) than Blink (go with your intuition). Most of us have not only programmed our intellect to distrust our intuition. We are taught from early in life to trust the external—trust authority, trust approval from others—and not trust the internal. We are also not taught how to distinguish intuition from feelings, and to trust feelings leads to doing what you want to do. That's why trusting your intuition can be frightening at first. No wonder there is the phenomenon of "The Quants"—whose native tongue is numbers and algorithms and systems, not personal relationships or human intuition.

Imagination is more closely associated with empathy and intuition than reason and logic. In order to follow Jesus, you have to "imagine" both yourself and who you are following. Sometimes it means looking closely in order to avoid slippery rocks or road blocks. Sometimes it is looking ahead into the distance and following a star. Most of all, it is trusting the Spirit for that voice of transparent authenticity. Intuition is the discernment to recognize false steps, wrong directions, and knowing how to follow God into every future.

The intuition to follow the light, to live in the light, is not measured by EQs or IQs but is a gift from God, that same gift that allows an ignorant sheep to follow the voice of the Shepherd, that allows the waves to obey the wave of Christ's hand, the gift that allows all of us to grow toward and sunbathe in the light.

Tip 6: Intimacy

Another *I* that "tips" the Truth of Christ in the world is the *I* of intimacy. God's Truth is about relationship, and not just any relationship but the kind of intimacy that demands humble confidence before our Creator. Intimacy revels in the revelation of the covenant—that Me/We exists for union with God. The truth of relationality, the intimacy of relationships grounded in agapic love, are hallmarks of a conceiver culture.

Intimacy is the thread that ties together our faith, binding our souls to God. The metaphor of binding is pivotal. Whether we are binding the commandments to our bodies in prayer through the tefillin, or binding the scriptures to our homes with the mezuzah, or binding the covenant to our hearts in the tallit with the tzitzit, the binding keeps Jewish people ever reminded that being in covenant relationship with God is the most important truth in life. What binds you to God?

The Jewish symbolism of the fringes (*tzitzit* in Hebrew) needs rediscovery. These "wings" were attached at the four corners of the tallit tunic. White threads intertwined and woven into knots with blue threads represent the intimate covenant relationship honored by the wearer. Numbers 15:37 gives instruction to the Hebrew people on how to knot and wear these tassels on their garments, as does Deuteronomy 22:12.

The covenant relationship in these passages is expressed in terms of the intimacy of marriage. To dishonor the covenant with God was to commit "adultery." To keep the covenant relationship is to be made whole in God and "healed," which the tzitzit or threaded tassels represent. The Hebrews believed that the coming Messiah would have the power to heal whoever touched these fringes of his tallit garment.

Jesus was particularly known for his healing powers in these wings. In the gospel of Mark[109] and Matthew,[110] people[111] would come from miles around to touch the hem or border that is the tzitzit or "wings" of his garment. And they were healed. "Who touched my clothes?" Jesus asked.[112] As a rabbi, Jesus wore the tallit with tzitzit throughout his ministry. It was this seamless robe that was bargained for with lots upon his death.

When Jesus needs his disciples the most, they aren't there. Yet he does not give up on them (or us). The last words Jesus speaks to his disciples (in Matthew) before the resurrection are, "Arise, let us go" (26:46 AT). He still wants us with him, even though we fail him and bail on him.

The tzitzit's blue thread symbolizes the divine covenant that is kept by God's people. Like the string around our finger, it is the string around our hearts that reminds us of our intimacy of faith and our initiation into the body of Christ and its mission in the world to heal in Jesus's name. Intimacy with God requires intimacy with each other. A conceiver society must be intimately and lovingly bound.

Tip 7: Innovation

Each of us bears the same mark of God's "designer label," but that mark looks different and plays out differently in each of our lives. That's why Jesus dared diverse metaphors to communicate the ways of his "House and Garden:" for example, yeast (leaven), mustard seed, a camel going through a "needle."

Innovators are edge dwellers, covenant cutters, trail blazers, seed planters. Innovators wield cutting-edge knives to live on the edge, not afraid to try new things, uncover fresh truths, pave new paths, deconstruct entrenched paradigms. Innovation requires veering, deviating, swerving, and sometimes even erring.

But the sword of innovation cuts both ways. Innovators also cut the strands and thread the needles that create new garments of understanding and action. Innovators carve stories and parables, cut stones that lay foundations, trim off injustice, and veer society toward mercy. Just as Jesus chose disciples who were both traditional and revolutionary, innovators are both traditional and revolutionary.

In the Hebrew tradition, the archangel Zadkiel is known as the angel of mercy. Zadkiel encourages people to pray, seek forgiveness, and forgive any who have hurt them. Zadkiel helps heal emotional wounds by salving painful memories and repairing broken relationships. In art, Zadkiel is often depicted holding a knife because Jewish tradition identifies Zadkiel as the angel who prevented Abraham from sacrificing his son. Zadkiel is the patron angel of people who forgive, and forgiveness is one of life's most creative and innovative endeavors.

All innovators have five things in common, according to recent research.[113] These five habits of mind are associating, questioning, observing, networking, and experimenting. Each one of these "habits" or "practices" gets stronger and more skillful the more seasoned one becomes. People and communities that have the highest "innovation premiums" also display these five habits of mind.

First, associating. This means the ability to match unconnected things, to connect the dots, to mix metaphors, to juxtapose difference, to bring opposites into relationship with one another. Associating requires broadening experiences to encounter that which is outside the tradition and tribe, or the mingling, stretching, and breaking of genres as an expressive response to challenges.

Second, questioning. This means loving questions, and asking childlike questions about why things are done like this and not like that, questions that unsettle settled opinions. This is different from the "questioning" of the Socratic Method, which Winston Churchill defined as "giving your friend his head in an argument and progging him into a pit by cunning questions."[114] It is also different from the famous Olympic question once asked by an Asian TV station of a losing athlete: "You are a national disgrace. Please comment." I was once asked to review a church video where United Methodist church members took to the streets to interview people on why they go to church. One of the questions was "Have you sensed the presence of church in your daily life?" You read that right. Not "Do you sense the presence of God in your daily life?" Not "Have you sensed the presence of Christ in your daily life?" But "Have you sensed the presence of church in your daily life?"

Innovative questioning is like that found in the book of Job, the book of the Bible with the most questions in it. The greatest questioner of all time was Jesus, who was famous for his questions. In fact, if you met Jesus on the street, he was more likely to ask you a question than tell you anything.[115] Innovative questioning reflects an openness to experience, and the extent to which a person is curious, imaginative, questioning, and creative, or conforming, unimaginative, predictable, and uncomfortable with novelty.

Third, a talent for observation. Jesus's signature phrase was "pay attention." One of the most powerful forces in the universe is self-delusion and denial. In this one phrase, once translated as "verily, verily I say unto thee" or more recently "I tell you the truth" but most accurately "pay attention," Jesus is rebuking our denials and illusions and inviting us to inhabit a state of semiotic awareness in which we see things as they actually are, not as we wish they were. Paying attention is what brings all things to life. Attention is what brings faith to life. Most important, attention is what brings Christ to life in peoples' lives.

Fourth, great networkers. Innovators hang around, not to cultivate contacts or to grab contracts but to get ideas and jam over wild and crazy ideas. Great networkers have a connection not to power structures but to creative people and communities that prize imagination and change.

Fifth, constant experimentation. Innovators love to fiddle and play. They also are masters of resourcefulness. When the crowd was so squeezed that a man who needed healing couldn't get through, some friends went up on the roof and lowered him on his mat through the tiles into the middle of the crowd, right in front of Jesus.[116] Innovators do not fear doing things differently. Innovators do not fear the change it takes to achieve a destiny. If you can't have a mountaintop experience, have a housetop experience, or even a laptop experience.

Conceiving the image of Jesus in our lives, we prepare ourselves not just for a Me life but for a We economy.

Conceiving as Seeding and Spreading the Gospel of a Jesus Economy (We)

It's the fruit that harbors the seed. And seeds are conceived in relationship with others. It is not enough to bear the fruit on the vine. It has to be low enough on the vine so that others can eat freely from it. It has to be given freely with abundance and without cost.

We are called to be fruitful, not just faithful. Fruitfulness is better language than faithfulness in talking about effective ministry. When God said "be fruitful and multiply," God was only calling us to reflect God's nature. God is fruitful and multiplies. The fertility of the universe is amazing: the universe contains 100 billion galaxies, each of which contains 100 billion stars of incredible uniqueness and diversity.

When a fruit ripens, if it's not eaten, it cannot seed another soil, it cannot nourish another. It merely rots and goes to waste. A conceiver society is abhorrent to waste. It bears fruit and puts that fruit to use within the world.

We need to be everyday conceivers, whether that means listening to a song, reading a good poem or chapter from a good book, gazing at a painting, or complimenting someone.

When narratives, liturgies, music, rituals, art are faithfully passed on from one generation to the next, all these creations are not stultifying doctrines allowing for no fresh-ups. Rather they are dynamic traditions open to alterations and participations, within parameters, of course. The Lord's Table is where we recommit ourselves, as branches of the Vine, to bear the fruit that is Christ. Everything we have is a gift made larger when we share it with someone else.

The ultimate art is not the conception/creation of a canvas or a composition but of a community, who creates upon it together the stories of their lives together.

A former student of mine had a grandmother, who in her nineties, with Alzheimer's working its way in her brain, was unable to remember who she was, but if you put a hook in her hand, she would start crocheting, and she would produce these squares, these magnificent squares, hundreds of them, all of which were given to the AIDS quilt foundation for children with AIDS. Every person on our planet has been given gifts of conception. To hold them in is one of the greatest sins we can commit.

The fruit the Lord expects of us is love—a love that accepts with him the mystery of the Cross, and becomes a participation in his self-giving—and hence the true justice that prepares the world for the Kingdom of God.
—Benedict XVI, *Jesus of Nazareth*

Everything we conceive out of our relationship with God will be an economy of movement forward in fruitfulness and flourishing. Only evil is associated with stagnation, inertia, nonrealization, and bureaucratic entanglement. Bearing fruit for a conceiver society is evangelism in its highest form.

Conceiving a "House and Garden" Economy

What makes the desert beautiful is that somewhere it hides a well.
—Antoine de Saint-Exupéry, *The Little Prince*

When Governor Meyner of New Jersey vetoed the nickname "The Garden State" in 1954, he argued that it was false advertising. Ninety-eight percent of New Jersey's citizens didn't work in agriculture. But the legislature overrode his veto and approved the nickname "Garden State" for the most densely populated state in the nation. And they did so for theologically good reasons. They countered that a "Garden State" could "grow" more than fruits and vegetables. It could grow health. It could grow commerce. It could grow technology. And they were right.

When we think about a paradigm shift from a consumerist economy to a "House and Garden" economy, a conceiver culture, we must tap our "garden memory." We all have a garden memory of God's first and last commands to "eat freely" and "drink freely." In a "House and Garden" economy, we consume in order to conceive. So what does it mean to pursue material wealth, not as an end in itself but as part of an ambition to bring about a better world? What does a "relational" conceiver society look like?

Vicki Robins suggests we should ask ourselves the following buy-this/birth-that questions before we purchase anything:

1. Does this item add to my experience of fulfillment or is it just clutter?

2. Is it worth my 'life energy,' the work time I've invested in earning the money to buy it?

3. Is having this item taking my life in the direction I want it to go?[117]

good questions

Whereas material goods are diminished by sharing,
the spiritual treasuries of knowledge and of beauty,
of poetry, music and the rest, by being shared
are not diminished but increased.

—Kathleen Raine, *The Land Unknown*

The etymology of "conception" is the Latin *concipere*, or to catch, receive, or wed. The etymology of "consume" is the Latin *consumere*, or to take completely. Imagine what has not been birthed but simply used up. It gives new meaning to the word *fulfillment*.

There is huge difference in creation and formation. What are your fillers? The "kingdom of heaven" is not a specific "place" that we "build" but a relationship that we enter into in which we are fulfilled by God, and conceive out of that fulfillment. A garden life is a meaning-filled life. A "House and Garden" world is a world in which we are caretakers and trustees, not owners. It is a world of collaborative consumption, where we're no longer defined as consumers by our personal possessions but by what we are part of, what we share, and the groups we belong to. It's a world in which the Me and the We collaborate and conserve and conceive together. The word *company*, in fact, is derived from the Latin words *cum* and *pane* meaning "breaking bread together." A conceiver "House and Garden" society is one that sets a table in the world for all people and perpetuates that food for generations forward. A conceiver society reorients our lives from personal consumption toward global citizenry.

So what do we do about our possessions . . . sell everything? Empty our checking accounts? How would I buy groceries? Pay for college? Make mortgage payments? Buy car insurance? Where would I sleep? Eat? A conserve-and-conceive economy must have some practical implications.

Some of these ideas have been tried already in secular communities. For example, in the Netherlands, "creative entrepreneurship" has been rejuvenating entire societies with an emphasis on the arts and technology. Imagine what disciples of the church could do if they began to think creatively. We must create churches that conceive in ways that allow old systems and stale habits to die, in order to birth new possibilities and generate new lives. "The seed that bears fruit must fall to the ground and die. You can't hold on to life without losing it" (John 12:24-25 AT). But the new life of the plant is a fuller life than that of the seed. The church today must be a countercultural force. But to be countercultural today, you are almost forced into being antichurch, since the church is so cultural and sold out to consumer culture. The call for a conceiver society is the call for churches to reclaim their position in the world as conceivers and innovators, givers and sharers.

How else can the church perpetuate the story of God's creation in conceiving a new society? It starts with becoming a garden of creativity, and having the faith and guts to try new ideas. Here are some that may give you a start:

- Buy things, not for their resale value but for their story value, and connect them to the greatest story.

- Buy children's gifts that stimulate their creativity from their minds, not that franchise Hollywood. Tell them the Story of eternal life, not the stories of everlasting strife.

- Perpetuate the Story of God's creation by living a "buy this, birth that" life that asks what you are creating with every purchase.

- Cultivate contentment with what you have.

- Develop a passion for another kind of fruit that fills and fulfills and share that fruit with others in your life. Be an evangelist for a "conceiver society."

- Make the church a Commons property where everyone has space to create, to grow, to conceive of new spaces.

- Let locals decide what works best for everyone involved in a conceiver society. Sometimes you need fences, sometimes open fields are best. Honor both fences and fields as God's property, and work together to make sure each conceives the good, the true, and the beautiful in life for all people.

- Organize "wild kitchens" . . . paid events where diners enjoy "rambling dinners of wild foraged foods" in private locales. In the Bay Area, for example, Rabins added delivery of food boxes to his menu of services. For $40 to $80 a box, subscribers get a steady supply of nettles, berries, and other wild foods without having to root around any further than their doorstep.

- Think about new forms of "Life Dollars" You earn credits by performing services or providing goods to one another. Some communities are experimenting with Community Exchange Systems (CES), or Local Economic Transfer Systems (LETS), or Time Dollars.

- Cultivate and conceive the "Loaf" principle. *Loaf* stands for local, organically produced, animal friendly, and fairly traded.

These are not the only ways, of course. Some of the above are only beginning to bear fruit within some societies and communities. But the good news of a Me/We gospel society based in a conserve-and-conceive paradigm is that you will always be open to new possibilities and creative ventures. The key to a conceiver society is not to know all of the answers but to create space and freedom to ask questions and to try new things.

Our mission in life? To "be fruitful and multiply." From our own fruit bearing, we will multiply the beauty, truth, and goodness of our "House and Garden" world. I have always thought that Augustine's great work, *The City of God*, should have been called the *Garden City of God*. God's kingdom is realized wherever a Me/We economy honors the King. It starts when Me and We together sit at the Lord's Table and turn the tables on evil.

Conclusion

A Me/We Social Gospel

A Redemption Story

It is hard to imagine this kind of optimism anymore, but in 1914, Andrew Carnegie gave two million dollars to establish the interreligious "Church Peace Union"—later renamed the Council on Religion and International Affairs. In giving this huge amount of money to the church, the equivalent of fifty million dollars in our day, Carnegie said: "It is too bad that the churches cannot have some funds for peace work. They could really do more than any other institution in existence."

That's optimism enough about the church. But the real optimism came when, in giving the funds, Carnegie displayed optimism about the world. He stipulated that if peace should come as a result of his investment, the trustees should use the money for the alleviation of poverty. And, if that should then come from their good works, they were free to take up other good causes at their discretion.

Thomas Reid (1710–1796), the philosopher of the Scottish Enlightenment, once chided his contemporary Samuel Johnson (1709–1784) for something he said. Johnson, the most quoted English author of all time except for Shakespeare, maintained that patriotism was the last resort of scoundrels. Reid mused that Johnson must have been unaware of the infinite possibilities and popularity of social reform and human betterment as a refuge for scoundrels, reprobates, and intellectual lightweights.

The way our best intentions can be misguided zeal is symbolized for me by The United Methodist building, the only nongovernment building on Capitol Hill. To this day, it remains the nerve center for liberal Christian activism and social gospel ideology. But its cornerstone is a reminder of how our

151

social justice "crusades" can be full of sound and fury, signifying little long-term change. The cornerstone is dedicated to the Methodist women active in the temperance movement, the great crusade for a booze-free America that was partly behind the building's construction in the first place.

There are two opposite statements in the same chapter about the poor, and both are right. Deuteronomy 15 states that if we followed God's commandments, "there need be no poor among you."

> In the land the LORD your God is giving you to possess as your inheritance, he will richly bless you, if only you fully obey the LORD your God and are careful to follow all these commands I am giving you today. . . . If anyone is poor among your fellow Israelites in any of the towns of the land the LORD your God is giving you, do not be hardhearted or tightfisted toward them. Rather, be openhanded and freely lend them whatever they need. . . . Give generously to them and do so without a grudging heart; then because of this the LORD your God will bless you in all your work and in everything you put your hand to.[1]

As soon as this declaration is made and an explanation given of what it will take to eliminate poverty, there is an opposite statement: "There will always be poor among you."[2] "There will always be poor people in the land. Therefore I command you to be openhanded toward your fellow Israelites who are poor and needy in your land."[3]

This is where we need to live, and move, and have our being—between the divine ideal and the human reality. God has given us all we need to live peaceably and harmoniously and abundantly with one another and with all that God has made. No child should have the blank pages of their life filled up with the fated text of a story that is over before it has begun, a book that opens only to shut, already closed to possibility and opportunity. But the nature of human failing and frailty is such that we need to speak out of both sides of our mouth and plant our feet firmly on both sides of where our mouth lies: Yes, there need be no poor among you, but yes, the poor you will always have with you.

Me/We attempts to show how our inherent human failings, our fixation on self-saving (filling) and self-promoting (dividing), have resulted from a world that needs to come back into a "House and Garden" relationship with God where, if we properly keep God's vineyard, we will be given our fill and can live in harmony with one another.

I once had a parishioner who was terribly ill, and she knew it. But she wouldn't let anyone help her beyond sympathizing with her on account of her sickness. She was afraid to let doctors treat her, and when we finally convinced her to seek treatment, they couldn't make her well, because she wouldn't tell them the truth about what was wrong with her. She was her own worst enemy.

So are we. We are a people who have fought God at every turn. The whole story of the Bible is God trying to get us to stop self-medicating and submit ourselves for healing. When you allow God to heal, you become whole. Only God can fill. Only God can heal. Only in relationship with our Creator can we look at each other and not see black or white, look inside and not see We or Me, and look at our world and not see "want" and "want not."

Turning the church inside-out like a sock so that its labels and logos talk to the world is not easy. Living a Me/We "House and Garden" gospel is not easy. But it is fun, filling, and full of surprises. In Me/We living, one plus one does not equal two but three or sometimes three thousand. This is why God's new social gospel is truly such good news.

Notes

Introduction

1. Rudyard Kipling, "The Ship That Found Herself," in *The Day's Work* (New York: Doubleday and McClure, 1898), 85.

2. Ibid., 98.

3. Ibid., 99.

4. Ibid., 105.

5. See *The Poverty and Justice Bible* (Contemporary English Version), which highlights in orange all the verses that refer to poverty and justice, about 2,000 to 3,000 verses (depending on who is counting what).

6. The conference website, which no longer exists, was www.asustainablefaith.com.

7. For recent attempts see Nicholas Wolterstorff, *Justice: Rights and Wrongs* (Princeton, NJ: Princeton University Press, 2008); *John Rawls, A Theory of Justice* (Cambridge, MA: Harvard University Press, 1971); and Richard Rorty (Walter Rauschenbusch's grandson), "Justice as a Larger Loyalty," *Ethical Perspectives* 4 (1997): 2:139–51.

8. Amartya Sen, *The Idea of Justice* (Cambridge, MA: Harvard University Press, 2009).

9. For more critique of the social justice movement, see Leonard Sweet and Frank Viola, *Jesus Manifesto* (Nashville: Thomas Nelson, 2010), 105–21.

10. See Origen on Matt 24:7 and on Matt 18:23. Origen, *Commentary on Matthew*, trans. John Patrick, ed. Allan Menzies (Buffalo, NY: Christian Literature Publishing, 1896).

11. We bandy about the word *fascist*—"fascist" this and "fascist" that. But in true fascist countries, demonstrators were tortured or killed; dissidents were rounded up and sent to concentration camps, then their ashes were delivered by registered post to relatives. *Fascist* is a word not to be used loosely.

12. Vladimir Tismaneanu, *The Devil in History: Communism, Fascism, and Some Lessons of the Twentieth Century* (Berkeley: University of California Press, 2012).

13. So argues Peter Singer of Princeton, whom the *New England Journal of Medicine* hailed as "perhaps the most influential living philosopher." The Dutch have already adopted Singer's recommendations. They allow doctors to kill infants, even those who have long life expectancies, based on their professional assessment that their lives wouldn't be "just lives" or "lives worth living." The premise that certain lives aren't "worth living" is a slippery slope, and one that I, for one, don't think Jesus would want us to get on.

14. 1 Cor 13:13.

15. Thanks to Scott Cairns for this reference.

16. Heb 2:17.

17. Dorothy L. Sayers, "The Meaning of Heaven and Hell," in *Introductory Papers on Dante: The Poet Alive in His Writings* (Eugene, OR: Wipf & Stock, 2006), 67.

18. Luke 12:48.

19. Tyler Wigg-Stevenson, *The World Is Not Ours to Save: Finding the Freedom to Do Good* (Downers Grove, IL: InterVarsity Press, 2014).

20. Cormac McCarthy, *Outer Dark* (New York: Vintage Books, 1993).

21. Fyodor Dostoyevsky, *The Brothers Karamazov*, trans. Constance Garnett (New York: The Macmillan Company, 1922), 54.

22. Robert Fogel, *The Fourth Great Awakening* (Chicago: University of Chicago Press, 2000).

23. Reinhold Niebuhr, *The Irony of American History* (Chicago: University of Chicago Press, 2008).

24. Tyler Wigg-Stevenson, *The World Is Not Ours to Save*, 18.

25. See Walter Rauschenbusch, *Prayers of the Social Awakening* (New York: Pilgrim Press, 1910).

26. Thanks to Paula Champion Jones for helping me develop this thought further.

27. Luke 17:21. The phrase is translated variously.

28. Eph 1:9-10.

29. 2 Sam 7:1-16.

30. 2 Sam 7:11.

31. Ray Oldenburg, *The Great Good Place*, 3rd ed. (Emeryville, CA: Marlowe & Company, 1999).

32. For the importance of the trinity in this discussion, see my book *The Three Hardest Words in the World to Get Right* (Colorado Springs, CO: Waterbrook Press, 2006).

33. See Magobe Ramose, *African Philosophy through Ubuntu* (Bloomington: Indiana University, 1999).

34. Charles A. Lindbergh, Entry for Sunday, July 2, 1939, in *The Wartime Journals of Charles A. Lindbergh* (New York: Harcourt Brace Jovanovich, 1970), 222.

35. Martin Luther, *Luther's Works*, ed. Helmut T. Lehmann and Martin E. Lehman, vol 38, *Word and Sacrament IV* (Philadelphia: Fortress, 1971), 241.

36. For more on the role of play, see my *The Well-Played Life: Why Pleasing God Doesn't Have to Be Such Hard Work* (Carol Stream, IL: Tyndale House Publishers, 2014).

1. "Only Connect"

1. Although the only miracle involving money is the temple tax. See Matt 17:24-27.

2. See 1 Cor 6:19 NIV.

3. Ps 100:3 NKJV.

4. Jas 1:17 AT.

5. Little Tiger Lyrics. http://www.lyricsmania.com/little_tiger_lyrics_tune-yards .html.

6. Deut 31:6 AT.

7. Quoted in Timothy Radcliffe, *What Is the Point of Being a Christian?* (London: Burns & Oates, 2005), 105.

8. James Hillman describes soul as the "middle ground between matter and spirit" (*Re-Visioning Psychology* [New York: Harper & Row, 1975], 3–50). Soul is the space between mind and body, event and experience, a relationship word that is neither matter or spirit but bound to both.

9. As quoted in Charlotte Sleigh, *Six Legs Better: A Cultural History of Mymecology* (Baltimore: Johns Hopkins University Press, 2007).

10. Twyla Tharp and others call this "collaborate individualism." See her book *The Collaborative Habit: Life Lessons for Working Together* (New York: Simon and Schuster, 2009), 7: "The real success stories of our time are about joint efforts: sports teams, political campaigns, businesses, causes."

11. 2 Cor 5:10.

12. Elizabeth Chapin is the source of this marvelous idea, if I remember correctly where I got it.

13. Jeffrey Stout, *The Flight from Authority: Religion, Morality, and the Quest for Autonomy* (Notre Dame, IN: University of Notre Dame, 1980), 49–50.

14. David Benner, *Soulful Spirituality: Becoming Fully Alive and Deeply Human* (Grand Rapids: Brazos Press, 2011), 138.

15. John Locke, *Essay Concerning Human Understanding* (Amherst, NY: Prometheus Books, 1995), 226–27.

16. Why did Adam fall? A suggestive answer is found in Augustine's *City of God*, where Augustine answered the question of "Why did Adam fall?" in this remarkable way: "He, by the drawing of kindred, yielded to the woman, the husband to the wife,

the one human being to the only other human being. . . . The man could not bear to be severed from his companion, even though it involved a partnership in sin." I was reminded of this by Karsten Harries, "The Shape of Modernity and the Future of Architecture," in *The Ethical Function of Architecture* (Cambridge, MA: MIT Press, 1997), 365.

17. Matt 10:29.

18. Ps 56:8.

19. Luke 12:7.

20. Matt 22:39, AT.

21. Larry Siedentop, *Inventing the Individual: The Origins of Western Liberalism* (London: Allen Lane, 2014); Richard Southern, *Western Society and the Church in the Middle Ages* (Harmonsworth, UK: Penguin, 1970).

22. Siedentop, *Inventing the Individual.*

23. Lee Siegel in *Against the Machine: Being Human in the Age of the Electronic Mob* (New York: Spiegel & Grau, 2008). See also my *Viral: How Social Networking Is Poised to Ignite Revival* (Colorado Springs, CO: WaterBrook Press, 2012).

24. With thanks to Facebook friend Przemek Bogdan for this multicultural reminder that the fixations of the West may not apply to the rest.

25. See Jonathan Steinberg, *All or Nothing: The Axis and the Holocaust, 1940–1943* (New York: Routledge, 1990).

26. For an alternative view, see Søren Kierkegaard:

> It is not the individual's relationship to the congregation which determines his relationship to God, but his relationship to God which determines his relationship to the congregation. Ultimately, in addition, there is a supreme relationship in which "the individual" is absolutely higher than the "congregation." . . . When a person first of all and qualitatively is an "individual," the concept "Christian congregation" (we would say "ekklesia") is secured as qualitatlively different from the "public," "many." . . . In community, the individual is; the individual is dialectically decisive as *prius* in order to form community; and in community the qualitative individual is essential and can at any instant become higher than "the community," namely, as soon as "the others" fall away from the idea [namely, the constituting commitment of the ekklesia]. (*Attack Upon Christendom*, trans. Walter Lowrie [Princeton, NJ: Princeton University Press, 1968], xxvii.)

27. See Robert Nisbet's "Quest for Community" (1953), arguably one of the most important sociological texts of the twentieth century. See Robert Nisbet, *Quest for Community* (Wilmington, DE: Intercollegiate Studies Institute, 2010).

28. Michael Walzer, *Spheres of Justice: A Defense of Pluralism and Equality* (New York: Basic Books, 1983), 31.

29. Jacob's household consisted of sixty-six people (Gen 46:26).

30. See the classic statement of this position in Lewis A. Coser, *The Functions of Social Conflict* (New York: Free Press, 1976).

31. Gene Knudsen, the founder of the Compassionate Listening Project, says "An enemy is someone whose story we really haven't heard." Quoted in Mark Brady, "What I've Learned from Listening," in *The Wisdom of Listening*, ed. Mark Brady (Boston: Wisdom Publications, 2003), 294.

32. David Guterson, "Surrounded by Water" in Annie Stine, ed., *The Earth at Our Doorstep: Contemporary Writers Celebrate the Landscapes of Home* (San Francisco: Sierra Club Books, 1996), 58.

33. Matt 25:40 AT.

34. C. S. Lewis, *The Screwtape Letters* (New York: HapperCollins, 2001), 145.

35. Mark 3:33-35 NRSV.

36. Richard Shweder, "After Just Schools: The Equality Difference Paradox" in *Just Schools: Pursuing Equality in Societies of Difference*, ed. Martha Minnow, Richard A. Shweder, and Hazel R. Markus (New York: Russell Sage Foundation, 2008), 254–90.

37. In his words, "ignoring the connection between culture and poverty is tantamount to self-censorship and indicates a basic failure of scholarship." Michael Jindra, "The Dilemma of Equality and Diversity," *Current Anthropology* 55 (June 2014).

38. See Bernard Williams's influential essay "The Idea of Equality," in *Problems of the Self* (1962; repr. New York: Cambridge University Press, 1973), 230–49, where he shows the necessity of refining the notion of equality and distinguishing equality of opportunity and equality of respect; the pursuit of both would lead to a "quite inhuman society" without working out refinements and balances.

39. Otherwise, why would so many books argue that "leaders are born, not made"?

40. The issue of inequality depends on an answer to three questions:

1. Is it morally wrong that people should be happy in different degrees? Is the possession by one person of more money or more talent or more intelligence than another morally offensive? Does anyone really want to live in a society where the umpire, or the cheerleader, or the groundskeeper makes the same money as Peyton Manning? Is excellence even possible in such an "egalitarian" society? Does anyone really want to live in Cuba?

2. Is it the business of the state to remedy purely moral wrongs?

3. If the answer to number two is yes, when might the remedy be worse than the disease? The moral issue of economics is not so much inequality but mobility. Are you stuck, or can you move? Are our communities less or more mobile than a generation ago? Are people more or less able to move between the rungs of the income ladder? Some people aren't stuck but don't want to move. Some people are quite content to be inert, victims of history, not participants in history or shapers of a story.

41. This is the thesis of Enrique Cambón's recent book, *Trinity: Model of Society* (Hyde Park, NY: New City Press, 2014).

42. The concept of *subsidiarity* is found in the Tenth Amendment, one of the Bill of Rights (1791), to the Constitution: "The powers not delegated to the United States by the Constitution, nor prohibited by it to the States, are reserved to the States respectively, or to the people."

43. G. K. Chesterton, *Heretics* (Rockville, MD: Serenity Publishers, 2009), 92.

44. Nick Spencer has issued a provocative ninety-page report, "Neither Private nor Privileged: The Role of Christianity in Britain Today," that can be found at www.theosthinktank.co.uk. Theos is the public theology think tank.

45. Oliver Letwin's *The Purpose of Politics* (London: Social Market Foundation, 1999) is a brilliant attack on "conviction politics" and "conviction politicians"—people on the left and right who want their values legalized in society.

46. Ruth Kelly, "Is Civilization the Only Value?" *TLS: Times Literary Supplement* (December 10, 1999): 27. See also Letwin, *The Purpose of Politics*.

47. Moses Finley, *The Ancient Economy* (Berkeley: University of California Press, 1973).

48. Wendell Berry, *A Timbered Choir: The Sabbath Poems, 1979–97* (Washington, DC: Counterpoint Publishing, 1998).

49. Fred D'Aguiar's book of poetry *British Subjects* opens with this poem. See D'Aguiar, *British Subjects* (Chester Springs, PA: Dufour Editions, 1993), 10.

50. Huston Smith, *The Soul of Christianity: Restoring the Great Tradition* (San Francisco: HarperSanFrancisco, 2005), xx.

51. Theo Hobson, *Reinventing Liberal Christianity* (Grand Rapids: Eerdmans, 2014).

52. Robert Southey, *Life of John Wesley*, 3rd ed., (London: Longman, Hurst, Rees, Orme, and Brown, 1820), 2:402.

53. Some of the most Machiavellian personalities in history have been ordained priests like Jozef Tiso, leader of Slovakia during World War II, or would-be priests.

54. Gal 2:20 NIV.

2. A Me/We Creation Story

1. Isaac Asimov, "Of What Use?" *Speaking of Research* (blog), March 23, 2012, http://speakingofresearch.com/2012/03/23/of-what-use/.

2. In *The Republic*, Plato likened the condition of humanity to that of prisoners in a cave. The fire behind them prevented them from seeing, since they were forced to stare ahead of themselves, while behind them people passed to and fro, their shadows thrown on to the wall of the cave at which the prisoners were staring. In this scenario, the prisoners take the shadows for reality. For Plato the goal of philosophy is the discovery of the true light of day outside.

3. This is how the Eastern Orthodox bishop Kallistos Ware in *The Orthodox Way* puts it: "We go out from the known to the unknown, we advance from light into darkness. We do not simply proceed from the darkness of ignorance into the light of knowledge, but we go forward from the light of partial knowledge into a greater knowledge which is so much more profound that it can only be described as the 'darkness of unknowing.' Like Socrates we begin to realize how little we understand. We see that it is not the task of Christianity to provide easy answers to every question, but to make us progressively aware of a mystery" (Crestwood, NY: St. Vladimir's Seminary Press, 1995).

4. A chapter entitled "Rules to Observe to Obtain the True Feeling which Must Be Ours in the Church Militant" includes the infamous Rule #13: "To be right in all matters, you must always be ready, before what I see as white, to believe that it is black if the hierarchical Church so decides."

5. Brian Kolodiejchuk, ed., *Mother Teresa: Come Be My Light: The Private Writings of the Saint of Calcutta* (New York: Doubleday, 2007). The editor is a member of the order of sisters and brothers founded by Mother Teresa.

6. T. S. Eliot, "East Coker," in *Four Quartets* (Orlando, FL: Harcourt, 1971), 27.

7. Even many humans who are dark don't like dark. A decade ago an Anglican bishop in Uganda (North Kigezi Diocese) confirmed 323 new Christians at All Saints Church in Rukungiri town. He specifically warned these converts to be on their guard against anyone who holds night prayers. In fact, such people should be shunned, because people who promote night praying promote sin because anything done under the cover of darkness is sinful. In spite of the fact that the bishop was himself of a dark color; and in spite of the fact that many early church fathers (e.g., St. Isaac the Syrian, 4th c.) said that prayer offered in the hours of darkness is the most powerful (the second most powerful is that prayer offered when we are fighting sleep): the association of black with evil triumphs. On June 25, 2006, The Reverend Edward Muhima also criticized African Christians who refuse to take their sick relatives to hospitals claiming they will survive on prayers. See Patson Baraire, "Bishop Condemns Night Prayers," *The Monitor* (Kampala), July 3, 2006, http://www.monitor.co.ug/artman /publish/news/Bishop_condemns_night_prayers.shtml (site discontinued).

8. Craig Koslofsky, *Evening's Empire: A History of the Night in Early Modern Europe* (Cambridge: Cambridge University Press, 2011).

9. 2 Cor 5:18 KJV.

10. Ps 91:5-6 AT.

11. Rev 22:16.

12. I want to thank British Jesuit Gerard W. Hughes for the inspiration of this metaphor of "two lights." See his *God in All Things: The Sequel to God of Surprises* (London: Hodder & Stoughton, 2003), 120–21, where he asks: "Can you imagine a modern politician trying to woo the electorate with the following manifesto: 'We promise all of you poverty of spirit, and, to some, actual poverty. Moreover, we shall make every effort to persuade you to come to a love of reproaches and contempt,

for this will lead you to humility, the highest of the virtues and the source of them all.' What a challenge for the spin doctors to make such a manifesto attractive to the electorate! A politician offering Lucifer's manifesto would have no need of spin doctors; the message would speak for itself: 'We promise you affluence, we promise you job security and status, leading to full-blown pride in your own importance and the importance of your nation'!"

13. Isa 45:3 NRSV.

14. Animals who are color-blind, like seals and dolphins, see things only in black and white. Birds and insects see colors better than humans do, so that the world looks very different to them than it does to us. They not only see our range but also the ultraviolet levels to which we are blind. Lestrels prey on voles by tracking their urine, which has chemicals that absorb ultraviolet light. Lestrels can use urine as runways as they come in for their "landing."

15. Of course, in times of war it can also symbolize the most dangerous hour of the day. See Alonso Cueto's *The Blue Hour*, trans. Frank Wynne (London: William Hienemann, 2012).

16. Very little research has been done on the impact of the color blue. The pineal produces the hormone melatonin, which tells us when it is day or night. The less light the pineal receives, the more melatonin it secretes. During long periods of darkness, an overproduction is thought to cause Seasonal Affective Disorder (SAD). Blue light is most effective in exciting melatonin into action. Are there spiritual ramifications to the benefit of blue light on the third-eye gland?

17. As quoted in Frederick Sherlock, "Temperance Arrows," in *Home Words for Heart and Hearth*, ed. Charles Bullock (London: "Home Words" Publishing Office, 1883), 22.

18. Simon Reid-Henry, "Chronology," *TLS: Times Literary Supplement* (April 21, 2006): 33.

19. David Prerau, *Seize the Daylight: The Curious and Contentious Story of Daylight Saving* (New York: Thunder's Mouth, 2005), xi–xiii.

20. For the "slumber and sleep" lifestyle, see Jesus's story of the man whose fields were overgrown with weeds because he "slumbered and slept" when he should have "waked up and worked" (Matt 13:24-30).

21. John 20:1.

22. This is the thesis of Allan Pritchard in *The Seventeenth Century: A Critical Survey* (Toronto: University of Toronto Press, 2006).

23. Mark 1:35.

24. John 20.

25. Sylvia Plath as quoted (from an unpublished typescript to a radio broadcast that was never delivered) in M. L. Rosenthal, *The New Poets: American and British Poetry since World War II* (New York: Oxford University Press, 1967), 81.

26. So says Michael Turner of the University of Chicago. Ron Cowen, "Embracing the Dark Side," *Science News* 173 (February 2, 2008): 74.

27. Brian Greene, "What is the Universe Made Of?" *Wired* (February 2007): 113.

28. Some scientists are even talking now about "mirror matter" or "shadow matter." In this theory, everything that exists has alongside it a parallel universe of "shadow matter" that shares our space but we just can't tell it's there. In this mirror world, every particle in our universe has a counterpart: mirror planets, mirror stars, mirror galaxies. This mirror matter world we know virtually nothing about but may be more important than the world of dark matter. The point? There is more to this world than meets the eye. There are other worlds that exist alongside our world. We all live by faith, and not by sight.

29. Isaac Watts, "There is a Land of Pure Delight," *The Methodist Hymnal: Official Hymnal of the Methodist Church* (Baltimore: Methodist Publishing House, 1939), 528.

30. Elizabeth McEwen Shields, *Beginners in God's World*, [words and music © 1925] *Worship and Conduct Songs for Beginners and Primaries for Use in the Church School, Sunday Session, Week Day Session, Vacation Session and the Home*, (Richmond, VA: Presbyterian Committee of Publication, 1929), 13.

31. Louis Armstrong, "What a Wonderful World."

32. See Denise Levertov's comment that a poet's work "is not to flood darkness with light so that darkness is destroyed, but to enter into darkness, mystery, so that it is experienced." Denise Levertov, "H. D.: An Appreciation," in her *The Poet in the World* (New York: New Directions, 1973), 246.

33. "Then the LORD said to Moses, 'Stretch out your hand toward the sky so that darkness spreads over Egypt—darkness that can be felt'" (Exod 10:21 NIV).

34. Phillips Brooks, "O Little Town of Bethlehem" (1868), in *The United Methodist Hymnal* (Nashville: The United Methodist Publishing House, 1989), 230.

35. Mark 15:33 AT.

36. John 20:1 AT.

37. Exod 20:21; Deut 4:11; 5:22; 2 Sam 22:10; 1 Kgs 8:12; 2 Chron 6:1; Pss 18:9; 97:2.

38. Nicholas Carr, *The Big Switch: Rewiring the World, from Edison to Google* (New York: W. W. Norton, 2008), 232.

39. Quoted in Alexander Theroux, *Laura Warholic: or, The Sexual Intellectual: A Novel* (Seattle: Fantagraphics, 2007), 506.

40. John Ruysbroeck, "The Book of the Sparkling Stone," in *Medieval Netherlands Religious Literature*, trans. Edmund Colledge (London: Heinemann, 1965), 95.

41. Louise Pollock, *National Kindergarten Manual* (Boston: DeWolfe, Fiske and Company, 1889), 13.

42. Gen 15:5 NIV.

43. Edward Thomas, "Out in the Dark," in *Collected Poems* (New York: Thomas Seltzer, 1921), 190.

44. For more monitoring and pictures of night pollution, see the National Park Service website, "Night Sky," last modified July 23, 2014, http://www2.nature.nps.gov/air/lightscapes/.

45. Ben Harder, "Light All Night: New Images Quantify a Nocturnal Pollutant," *Science News* 169 (March 18, 2006): 171, http://www.sciencenews.org/articles/20060318/bob10.asp.

46. Ibid.

47. German writer/artist Peter Weiss, as quoted in William Sloane Coffin, *The Collected Sermons* (Louisville: Westminster John Knox, 2008), 497.

48. John Henry Newman, "The Pillar of Cloud," in *Hymns of the Christian Church*, vol 45, part 2, The Harvard Classics (New York: P. F. Collier & Son, 1909–14).

49. Macrina Wiederkehr, *A Tree Full of Angels: Seeing the Holy in the Ordinary* (San Francisco, Harper & Row, 1990).

50. Quoted in Thomas J. Green, *Drinking from a Dry Well* (Notre Dame, IN: Ave Maria Press, 1991), 54.

51. Iain Matthew, *The Impact of God: Soundings from St. John of the Cross* (London: Hodder and Stoughton, 1995), 57.

52. R. S. Thomas, "Via Negativa," in *Collected Poems 1945-1990* (London: Orion Books, 2000), 220. Copyright © R. S. Thomas 1993.

53. Ps 100:3 NIV, with the alternate wording of the last phrase as noted in footnote b.

54. Rainer Maria Rilke, "I Have Many Brothers," in *Selected Poems of Rainer Maria Rilke: A Translation from the German and Commentary by Robert Bly*, trans. Robert Bly (New York: Harper and Row, 1981), 15.

55. Rainer Maria Rilke, "You Darkness, That I Come From," in Bly, *Selected Poems of Rainer Maria Rilke*, 21.

56. W. H. Auden, "In Memory of Sigmund Freud," in *Collected Poems*, ed. Edward Mendelson (New York: Vintage Books, 1991), 276.

57. This story is told by James D. Dennis, "Meditations on Mary and Simeon," December 11, 2005, http://www.msumc1.org/NewSermonPage/PDFSermon11Dec05.pdf.

58. Quoted in Nicholas Sagovsky, *On God's Side: A Life of George Tyrrell* (New York: Oxford University Press, 1990), 110.

59. Robert D. Dale, *Seeds of the Future: Growing Organic Leaders for Living Churches* (St. Louis, MO: Lake Hickory Resources, 2005), 98.

60. Eph 5:8-9 NRSV.

61. 1 John 2:10 NRSV.

62. Gen 1:2–3:1; John 1:5.

63. Ps 139:12 NASB.

64. This is sometimes called the apophasis/apophatic tradition of the unsaying God: "[Apophatic theology] is speech about God which is the failure of speech; it is failure in the sense of speech slowing to a halt in awed wonder before the presence of what is always more than one can say." Denys Turner, *The Darkness of God: Negativity in Christian Mysticism* (Cambridge: Cambridge University Press, 1995).

65. I steal this phrase from Novalis's "Hymnen an die Nacht" (1800) or "Hymns to the Night."

66. John Donne, "A Hymn to Christ, at the Author's Last Going into Germany," in *Poems of John Donne*, vol. 1, ed. E. K. Chambers (London: Lawrence and Bullen, 1896), 193–94.

67. Quoted in *Off the Page: Writers Talk about Beginnings, Endings, and Everything in Between*, ed. Carole Burns (New York: Norton, 2008).

68. Gen 1:2 NRSV.

69. Peter Barnes, "The Slaughterman," in his *The Spirit of Man and More Barnes' People: Seven Monologues* (London: Methuen Drama, 1990), 61.

70. Lawrence Krauss, *The Physics of Star Trek* (New York: Basic Books, 2007), 38.

71. John 1:9.

72. Ps 4:6 KJV.

73. 1 Pet 2:9 NRSV.

74. Ps 36:9.

75. Ps 37:6; Isa 10:17; 51:4; Hos 6:5.

76. Matt 6:22-23; Luke 11:34-36; John 9:4; 12:46-47; 2 Cor 6:14; 1 Thess 5:4-8; 1 John 2:10.

77. Isa 11:5-6 AT.

78. Eph1:8-12 AT.

79. William Dunbar, "Unto Us a Son Is Born," as quoted in Benjamin Francis Musser, "The Chaucer of Scotland," *Franciscan Poets* (New York: Macmillan, 1933), 9.

80. Paul Gerhardt, "Now All the Woods Are Sleeping," ("Nun Ruhen alle Wälder"), in *The Chorale Book for England,* trans. Catherine Winkworth (London: Longman, Green, Longman, Roberts, and Green, 1863), no. 169.

3. A Me/We Economy

1. Deut 20:19 GNT.

2. Paul Ginsborg, *The Politics of Everyday Life: Making Choices, Changing Lives* (New Haven: Yale University Press, 2005), 61.

3. John Hudson, "Lawyer, Praise Thyself," *TLS: Times Literary Supplement* (December 12, 2008): 28.

4. Victoria de Grazia, *Irresistible Empire: America's Advance through Twentieth-Century Europe* (Cambridge, MA: Harvard University Press, 2006). "Incremental consumption, especially in the rich countries of the world and especially after 1945, was quite breathtaking: by 1998 24 trillion US dollars were being spent worldwide in private and public consumption, twice the figure for 1975, and six times that of 1950. The overall effect on global ecology was bound to be startling. Few of the environmental changes of the twentieth century were entirely new (the human-induced thinning of the ozone layer was one), but the scale and intensity of pressure on the environment were quite unprecedented." John McNeill, *Something New Under the Sun* (London: Allen Lane, 2000), 4, 360, as referenced by Paul Ginsborg, *The Politics of Everyday Life: Making Choices, Changing Lives* (New Haven: Yale University Press, 2005), 37.

5. Ps 22 AT.

6. Rom 3:23 NRSV.

7. Jer 5:4.

8. Isa 9:12-16.

9. Prov 28:16.

10. Deut 8:17 NRSV.

11. Luke 8:1-3.

12. Richard Conniff, *The Natural History of the Rich: A Field Guide* (New York: W. W. Norton, 2002), 135–36.

13. E. Stanley Jones, *Christ's Alternative to Communism* (New York: Abingdon Press, 1935), 35.

14. Max Weber, *The Protestant Ethic and the Spirit of Capitalism* (London: Unwin, 1930), 181.

15. For a scholarly look at the impact of materialist consumption on the development of identity, see Anthony Giddens, *Modernity and Self-Identity*: "The consumption of ever-novel goods becomes in some part a substitute for the genuine development of self; appearance replaces essence as the visible signs of successful consumption come actually to outweigh the use-values of the goods and services in question themselves" (Stanford, CA: Stanford University Press, 1991), 198.

16. As quoted by Gregory Wolfe, "Thirty Seconds Away," *Image* 63 (Fall 2009).

17. Quoted in Robert Southey, *The Life of Wesley* (Charleston, SC: Bibliolife, 2009). Wesley had the second-highest earned income of any eighteenth-century Englishman but vowed not to die without having given it all away. A donor to Drew had this lifetime motto regarding stocks: "Buy low, give-away high." a twenty-first-century version of Wesley's "Make/Save/Give all you can."

18. The Census Bureau reported that there were more than 1.4 billion credit cards in 2004, for 164 million cardholders—an average of 8.5 cards per cardholder.

19. In his early theological study of AA, Ernest Kurtz concludes that the word *alcoholic* could very well serve as a metaphor for the term *modern man*. See Ernest Kurtz, *Not-God: A History of Alcoholics Anonymous* (Center City, MN: Hazelden Educational Services, 1979), 229.

20. Christopher Jamison, "If Consumerism Is Now the Native Culture, Church Leaders Condemn It Outright at Their Peril," *The Tablet* (December 31, 2011): 7. He ends his essay with "Why should the devil have all the best shops?"

21. Samuel Johnson, Tuesday, 8 May 1781, as quoted in *Boswell's Life of Johnson*, ed. George Birkbeck Hill, rev. and enlarged edition by L. F. Powell (New York: Oxford University Press, 1934), 1:105–6.

22. A "sharing economy" is the theme of Beth Buczynski, *Sharing Is Good: How to Save Money, Time and Resources through Collaborative Consumption* (Gabriola, B.C.: New Society Publishers, 2013). See also Rachel Botsman and Roo Rogers, *What's Mine Is Yours: The Rise of Collaborative Consumption* (New York: Harper Business, 2010).

23. Lee Eisenberg, *Shoptimism: Why the American Consumer Will Keep on Buying No Matter What* (New York: Free Press, 2009).

24. I get the phrase via Charles Handy, *Hungry Spirit* (New York: Broaday Books, 1998), 45–46.

25. Actual title: *Worship Resources for the Millenium*, publication of Churches Together in England (London: New Start, 2000), quoted in Noreena Hertz, *The Silent Takeover: Global Capitalism and the Death of Democracy* (New York: Free Press, 2001), 116.

26. Even the Communists couldn't beat it. It outlasted them and now flourishes in the ruins of their regimes. And the Market as God is omnipresent, it is everywhere, turning the whole of creation into a commodity. It dominates every area of life. For instance, traditional religions have regarded human beings as sacred, but long ago the Market reduced them to an inventory of spare parts to be sold a piece at a time—blood, sperm, fertilizable eggs, and no doubt human genes will soon be added. And if in spite of having bought a spanking new body you are still unhappy, the Market can sell you peace of mind and personal fulfilment offered by some psychological guru or life-style consultant. Just like the Christian God, the Market loves sinners. . . . The Market God is insatiable: its motto is "there is never enough." (Colin Morris, *Things Shaken—Things Unshaken: Reflections on Faith and Terror* [London: Epworth, 2006], 126–27)

27. Rev 13:10.

28. For more on these three "transcendentals of being," see my book *The Three Hardest Words in the World to Get Right* (Colorado Springs, CO: WaterBrook Press, 2006).

29. Ps 66:12 AT.

30. See the chapter by Pat Murphy and Faith Morgan of the Arthur Morgan Institute for Community Solutions in *State of the World 2013: Is Sustainability Still Possible?* (Washington, DC: Island Press, 2013).

31. See, for example, the whole Livesimply campaign of the Roman Catholic Church, which was adopted by thirty-nine Catholic organizations in England and Wales, with its inspiration from Pope Paul VI's 1967 encyclical *Populorum Progressio*.

32. Quoted in Paul Ginsborg, *The Politics of Everyday Life: Making Choices, Changing Lives* (New Haven: Yale University Press, 2005), 61.

33. Ibid., 67. The simplicity movement can be so legalistic, and thus hypocritical, as evidenced in the anticapitalist rant of Judith Levine in *Not Buying It: My Year without Shopping* (New York: Free Press, 2006). I can completely understand why she would exempt quality coffee while limiting herself to the "necessities" of daily life. Her list of "necessities" include high-speed DSL, cable television, "organic French roast coffee beans," etc. I completely understand these exemptions in a move toward simplicity, but I'm not sure tea drinkers will. Or wine afficionados. Or, well, you can fill in the blanks with your own guilty pleasures that you'd redefine as part of the "simple life."

34. Gen 1:3.

35. Gen 1:31 NRSV.

36. See Leonard Sweet, *So Beautiful* (Colorado Springs, CO: David C. Cook, 2009), 59.

37. Robert Gottlieb, *Balanchine: The Ballet Maker* (New York: HarperCollins, 2007).

38. Luke 6:35 NRSV.

39. See the work by one of the founders of string theory, Michio Kaku, *Parallel Worlds: A Journey Through Creation, Higher Dimensions, and the Future of the Cosmos* (New York: Doubleday, 2005), esp. "The Multiverse," 111–283.

40. We learned this concept a long time ago from Amos Wilder, *Early Christian Rhetoric* (London: SCM Press, 1964), 14.

41. Ralph Waldo Emerson, "The Conservative," in *Nature: Address and Lectures* (Boston: Munroe, 1849).

42. John 5:17 AT.

43. See Leonard Sweet, *The Well-Played Life: Why Pleasing God Doesn't Have to Be Such Hard Work* (Carol Stream, IL: Tyndale House Publishers, 2014).

44. Patrick Kavanagh, "Miss Universe," in *Collected Poems* (New York: Penguin Classics, 2005), 231.

45. René Descartes, *Discourse on the Method of Rightly Conducting the Reason and Seeking Truth in the Sciences*, in his *Discourse on Method and Meditations*, trans. Laurence J. Lafleur (Indianapolis, IN: Bobbs-Merrill, 1960), 45.

46. Twyla Tharp, *The Collaborative Habit: Life Lessons for Working Together* (New York: Simon & Schuster, 2009), 142.

47. John Gray uses the phrase "homo rapiens" in his *Straw Dogs: Thoughts on Humans and Other Animals* (London: Granta Books, 2002), 151, 184.

48. Another nonfluid way of looking at it is to envision three "natural sinks": earth, sea, sky, all three suffering from unrestrained consumption. Car manufacturers annually spend over twice the billions of dollars to promote their vehicles as the federal government spends on improving public transport.

49. Ps 8:3 NKJV.

50. Czeslaw Milosz, *Proud to Be a Mammal* (New York: Penguin, 2010), 84.

51. Ps 36:6-7 NRSV.

52. Gen 9:16 AT.

53. Wendell Berry, *The Way of Ignorance* (Emeryville, CA: Shoemaker & Hoard, 2005), 135.

54. Gen 3:15 AT.

55. John 3:14 NIV.

56. With thanks to Jorge Findley for helping me develop this connection.

57. Roger Scruton argues in *Green Philosophy* (London: Atlantic, 2012) that the "natural bedfellow" of environmentalism is conservatism, for "conservatism and conservation are two aspects of a single long-term policy." Environmentalism is conservative policy, since it embodies "an approach to environmental problems in which local affections are made central . . . and in which homeostasis and resilience, rather than social reordering and central control" are primary.

58. Johan Verstraeten, "Economics with a Human Face," *The Tablet* (February 25, 2012): 12.

59. Elinor Ostrom, *Governing the Commons: The Evolution of Institutions for Collective Action* (Cambridge, MA: Cambridge University Press, 1990).

60. I started out calling it *commons-ism* but abandoned that for obvious reasons of misunderstanding.

61. People as diverse as Bill McKibben and James Davison Hunter are using this phrase "the Commons." For McKibben and Hunter see *Thrift and Thriving in America* (New York: Oxford University Press, 2011). For Hunter, see *To Change the World: The Irony, Tragedy, and Possibility of Christianity in the Late Modern World* (New York: Oxford University Press, 2010).

62. Jonathan Rowe, *Our Common Wealth: The Hidden Economy That Makes Everything Else Work* (San Francisco: Berrett-Koehler, 2013).

63. See Kevin Treston, *Walk Lightly upon the Earth*, (Wilston, Queensland: Creative Enterprises, 2003).

64. Quoted in Clive Sinclair, "Heaven Blazing into the Head," *TLS: Times Literary Supplement* (September 20, 2013).

65. Metropolitan Life Insurance Co. Survey, as reported by David Pearce Snyder, "A New Middle-Class Mind-Set," *Trend Letter* (January 2010): 3.

66. Matt 6:21 NIV.

67. Rom 8:21-23.

68. Exod 20:4 AT.

69. 1 Kgs 6:28 NKJV—"he overlaid the cherubim with gold."

70. Nathaniel Hawthorne, "Earth's Holocaust," in *Moses from an Old Manse*, vol. 10 of the Centenary Edition of the Works of Nathaniel Hawthorne (Columbus: The Ohio State University Press, 1974).

71. Jay Griffiths, *Kith: The Riddle of the Childscape* (London: Hamish Hamilton, 2013).

72. Igor Sikorsky, *The Message of the Lord's Prayer* (New York: C. Scribner's Sons, 1942), 48.

73. Ambrose as found in M. Douglas Meeks, *God the Economist* (Minneapolis, MN: Fortress Press, 2000), 107.

74. U. S. Catholic Bishops: Office of the Catechism, *The Catechism of the Catholic Church*, Part 3, Section 2: "The Ten Commandments," Article 7: "The Seventh Commandment," VI: "Love for the Poor," accessed June 7, 2006, http://www.usccb.org/catechism/text/pt3sect2chpt2art7.htm.

75. With thanks to friend Rimes McElveen for helping me formulate this phrase.

76. The bombing of Dresden was memorialized in Kurt Vonnegut's *Slaughterhouse Five*: "All of this happened, more or less. The war parts, anyway, are pretty much true. One guy I knew really was shot in Dresden for taking a teapot that wasn't his. Another guy I knew really DID threaten to have his personal enemies killed by a hired gunman after the war. And so on. I've changed all the names. I really did go back to Dresden with Guggenheim money (God love it) in 1967. It looked a lot like Dayton, Ohio, more open spaces than Dayton has. There must be tons of human bone meal in the ground." (New York: Dell, 1991), 1.

77. Paul Bahn and John Flenley, *Easter Island, Earth Island* (London: Thames and Hudson, 1992), 213.

78. Ibid., 218.

79. As quoted in Paul Ginsborg, *The Politics of Everyday Life: Making Choices, Changing Lives* (New Haven: Yale University Press, 2005), 85. The actual Shelley quote is "the pains and pleasures of his species become our own." Percy Bysshe Shel-

ley, "A Defence of Poetry," in *Shelley's Poetry and Prose*, 2nd ed., ed. Donald H. Reiman and Neil Fraistat (New York: W. W. Norton, 2002), 517.

80. Matt 11:19 AT.

81. Rom 14:17 AT.

82. Roy F. Baumeister, Kathleen D. Vohs, Jennifer L. Aaker, Emily N. Garbinsky, "Some Key Differences between a Happy Life and a Meaningful Life," *Journal of Positive Psychology* 8, no. 6 (2013): 505–16.

83. For a philosophical elaboration of this difference, and what it means to "personalize the future" (a phrase I love), see Samuel Scheffler, *Death and the Afterlife* (Oxford: Oxford University Press, 2014).

84. Julie Nelson suggests the economy as a "beating heart" that "brings body and soul together." Just as the human heart provides nourishment to the body, so does the economy circulate money, goods, and services to maintain good health. Moreover, a person's heart can also be interpreted in abstract terms as the centre of love, compassion, and courage; similarly, she says, an economy can be seen as caring, consisting of people and institutions who are concerned for the welfare of others and who will act to help those in need (*Economics for Humans* [Chicago: Chicago University Press, 2006], 58–60).

85. One that serves not just companies or shareholders but the interests of the people and planet.

86. Gen 1:28.

87. Ps 107:9; Luke 1:53.

88. We think we are rich with choice, rich with freedoms never dreamed of by the ordered hierarchies of premodernity, or Fordist fill-in-the-blanks bureaucracies of modernity. But apart from the questions of what are we using our freedom for, or what are we doing with all our "choices," there is the nagging suspicion that this "choice culture" is mainly an illusion. In fact, the quality of our choices are like those "first class" passengers are required to make by the airlines: beef or chicken. Economist Juliet Schor argues that people's consumption patterns and preferences adjust to the environment, not to their choices. In the market, you want what you have, you don't have what you want.

89. For Rowan Williams's argument along these lines, see Timothy Radcliffe, "Learning Spontaneity," *What Is the Point of Being a Christian?* (New York: Continuum, 2005), 44–45.

90. I first proposed the trajectory of these thoughts in *AquaChurch: Essential Leadership Arts for Piloting Your Church in Today's Fluid Culture* (Loveland, CO: Group Publishing, 1999), 219–21:

> *We are conceivers, all!* Here is the *imago dei* in us: knowing God we conceive, knowing God we ourselves are birthers of the image of God. All existence is a participation in the existence of the Creator. The more knowledge we bear, the more knowing we do, the more we bear our Creator's image, the more we do our Creator's will.

171

Or let me tease you a bit by translating this into the dictionary of economics. One of the problems in our economic system today is that we have listened to Adam Smith, who got so much right except this one mistake: He based an economic system on human self-interest as the driving, motivating force behind human endeavor. That is why the "free" market is advantageous for the rich, the clever, the gifted, the inventive, the educated. But it is disadvantageous to the poor and uneducated, the less favored and more helpless. The "free" market frees the rich but exploits the poor.

What if we were to base an economic system on conceiving—not on self-interest—as the driving, motivating force underlying human action? What if conception rather than consumption were to govern the marketplace? What if capitalism were to be so conceived that the free play that is now allowed to selfishness in economic pursuits were allowed to conceiving? What if the U.S. tax code were as biased toward conception as it is now toward consumption?

We would become a society of conceivers rather than consumers. In other words, we would behave artistically. We would become artists.

91. Elsewhere Meister Eckhart says, "From all eternity God lies on a maternal bed giving birth. The Essence of God is birthing," *Meditations with Meister Eckhart*, introduction and versions by Matthew Fox (Santa Fe, NM: Bear, 1982), 88. See also Matthew Fox, *Wrestling with the Prophets: Essays on Creation Spirituality and Everyday Life* (San Francisco: HarperSanFrancisco, 1994), 93: "What does God do all day long, God gives birth." "What good is it to me for the creator to give birth to his/her Son if I do not also give birth to him in my time and my culture?" (Fox, *Meditations with Meister Eckhart*, 81).

92. Saint Ambrose, *Commentary on Luke's Gospel*, 2:26.

93. "My children, I am in terrible pain until Christ may be seen living in you" (Gal 4:19 CEV).

94. Edith Sitwell, "Holiday," in *The Collected Poems of Edith Sitwell* (New York: Vanguard Press, 1954), 301

95. John Newton, Letter VIII, January 19, 1763, in his "An Authentic Narrative, Etc.," in *The Works of the Rev. John Newton, Late Rector of the United Parishes of St. Mary Woolnoth and St. Mary Woolchurch-Haw, Lombard Street, London; To Which Are Prefixed Memoirs of His Life, by the Rev. R. Cecil, A.M.* (Edinburgh: Printed for Thomas Nelson, 1837), 20.

96. Matt 7:15-16 NRSV.

97. While Aristotle, and particularly Plato, originated the idea of the transcendentals, starting with the One, good, and true, Aquinas brought them into the realm of theology with five characteristics. The final three "true, good, beautiful" can be attributed to Marsilio Ficino who resurrected them in his *Commentaries* on Plato's Dialogues. Diderot later compared the good, true, and beautiful to the Father, Son, and Holy Spirit.

98. See Galatians.

99. Gal 5:22-23 NRSV.

100. Thanks to Bonnie Fackre-Cochise for helping me formulate this.

101. John 15:5 AT.

102. David Bosch, *A Spirituality of the Road* (Scottdale, PA: Herald Press, 1979), 42.

103. Edward Hadas, "Looking through the Eye of the Needle," *The Tablet* (April 1, 2006): 29.

104. Nathan Wolfe, *The Viral Storm: The Dawn of a New Pandemic Age* (New York: Times Books, 2012).

105. Martin Luther, *Luther's Works*, ed. Franklin Sherman and Helmut T. Leh-mann, vol. 48, *Letters I* (Philadelphia: Concordia and Fortress Press, 1963), 280–82.

106. Hos 2:14-16 AT.

107. Mark 9:24 NKJV.

108. Richard Pipes, *VIXI: Memoirs of a Non-Belonger* (New Haven: Yale University Press, 2004).

109. Mark 5:25; 6:56.

110. Matt 9:20.

111. In Matthew and Mark 5:25 a specific woman.

112. Mark 5:30.

113. See *The Innovator's DNA*, a follow up to Christensen's earlier volume (*The Innovator's Dilemma*) that popularized the concept of "disruptive innovation." Clay Christensen, Jeff Dyer, and Hal Gregersen in *The Innovator's DNA* (Boston: Harvard Business Press, 2011).

114. Quoted in Christopher Coker, "Afghan Fiction," *TLS: Times Literary Supplement* (November 20, 2009): 24.

115. Conrad Gempf has written a whole, wonderful book on this one fact called *Jesus Asked* (Grand Rapids: Zondervan, 2003). See also David Dark's *The Sacredness of Questioning Everything* (Grand Rapids: Zondervan, 2009).

116. Luke 5:19.

117. See the chapter "Enough—The Time Cost of Stuff" in John de Graaf, ed., *Take Back Your Time: Fighting Overwork and Time Poverty in America* (San Francisco: Berrett-Koehler, 2004).

Conclusion

1. Deut 15:4-5, 7-8, 10 NIV.

2. John 12:8 AT.

3. Deut 15:11 NIV.

CPSIA information can be obtained at www.ICGtesting.com
Printed in the USA
LVOW12s0723100914

403284LV00001B/3/P